Springs and Stones
Women of Inheritance

Rachel Underwood

Copyright © 2025 by Rachel Underwood. All rights reserved.
No portion of this book may be reproduced in any form without the written permission from the author, except as permitted by the Copyright Act 1968.

Trade paper back ISBN: 978-1-7643692-0-6
ePUB ISBN: 978-1-7643692-1-3
1st edition, 2025, printed in Australia

Scripture quotations taken from the Holy Bible, New International Version® (NIV®). Copyright© 1973, 1978, 1984, 2011 by Biblica, Inc.™ Used by permission. All rights reserved worldwide.

Scripture quotations taken from the Amplified® Bible (AMP),Copyright © 1954, 1958, 1962, 1964, 1965, 1987 by The Lockman Foundation. Used by permission. All rights reserved.

Scripture quotations are from the ESV®Bible (The Holy Bible, English Standard Version®), Copyright © 2001 by Crossway, a publishing ministry of Good News Publishers. Used by permission.All rights reserved.

Scripture quotations taken from the New King James Version®. Copyright © 1982 by Thomas Nelson. Used by permission. All rights reserved.

Scripture quotations taken from the Holy Bible, New Living Translation, Copyright © 1996, 2004, 2015 by Tyndale House Foundation. Used by permission of Tyndale House Publishers, Inc., Carol Stream, Illinois 60188. All rights reserved.

Scripture quotations taken from The Message. Copyright © 1993, 2002. 2018 by Eugene H.Peterson. Used by permission of NavPress. All rights reserved. Represented by Tyndale House Publishers, Inc.

Scripture quotation taken from the Amplified® Bible, Classic Edition (AMPC). Copyright © 1954, 1958, 1962, 1964,1965, 1987 by The Lockman Foundation. Used by permission. All rights reserved.

Scripture quotations marked TPT are taken from The Passion Translation®. Copyright © 2017, 2018, 2020 by Passion & Fire Ministries, Inc. Used by permission. All rights reserved. ThePassionTranslation.com.

Cover image: AI-generated photo by JESUS_is_our_only_HOPE (Arnie Bragg, Pixabay, Sept 4, 2024).

I dedicate this book to my beloved husband,
my children, grandchildren,
the generations to come

and

To every beautiful woman who sees herself in the stories
within these pages

This inheritance is yours!

For the Lord is good
and His love endures forever;
His faithfulness continues
through all generations.

Ps 100:5 NIV

Contents

Foreword   1

Part 1
Gods Plan for Inheritance

   1. Discovering Our Inheritance   7

   2. Springs in a Dry Land   21

   3. Courage to Speak Up!   33

Part 2
Encounters at a Well

   4. The God who Sees   45

   5. Encounter at the Well   57

Part 3
Daughters of Today

   6. Simple Faith   69

   7. Free Indeed   77

   8. Peace in the Valley   85

Part 4
Generational Wells

 9. Prayer Warrior 93

 10. Language of Love 101

 11. My Story 109

 12. Honouring God 131

 13. Grace 139

 14. Our Youngest Olive Shoot 149

 15. A Mother's Prayer 159

 16. The Prodigal's Inheritance 163

 17. War over the Seed 183

Part 5
Lineage of Grace

 18. From Walls to Legacy 195

 19. Justice in the Shadow of Shame 203

 20. Crowned in Grace 217

 21. Carrying the Promise of Heaven 227

 22. Harvesting what she didn't Sow 237

Part 6
Your Invitation!

23. Invitation to the Springs	251
24. Final Blessing	257
Acknowledgements	261
Endnotes	265

Foreword

This book, Springs and Stones, flows from my delight in God's presence. As I sat in stillness and meditated on His Word, He spoke gently and powerfully to my heart. He whispered truths I felt led to share with you. These pages tell the stories of faithful women who received their inheritance and invites you to discover yours too.

There's one verse that has walked me through many seasons. It has become a steady anchor for my heart.

> Delight yourself in the Lord, and *He* will give you the desires of your heart.
>
> Ps 37:4 ESV

I want to encourage you to take time to delight in Him. As you do, He will gently place His desires in your heart and water you with His Word.

He will begin to reveal a purpose and a plan. It is far greater than you could have imagined. There is a promise in His Word for you:

> Now to Him who is able to do exceedingly abundantly above all that we ask or think, according to the power that works in us...
>
> Eph 3:20 NKJV

He knows your name. He knows your story. And He's not finished writing it yet. David, the Psalmist writes:

> Your eyes saw my unformed body; all the days ordained for me were written in your book before one of them came to be.
>
> Ps 139:16 NIV

There is purpose woven into every part of your journey. He is present in every chapter of your story! There is a promise found in Romans 8:28 AMP:

> And we know [with great confidence] that God [who is deeply concerned about us] causes all things to work together [as a plan] for good for those who love God, to those who are called according to His plan and purpose.

A paraphrase of the Bible called *The Passion Translation* puts it like this,

> So we are convinced that every detail of our lives is continually woven together for good, for we are His lovers who have been called to fulfil his designed purpose.

With love,

Rachel

Part 1
Gods Plan for Inheritance

Chapter 1

Discovering Our Inheritance

A Journey through the Word

Inheritance is a thread woven throughout the entire Word of God!

This chapter invites us to explore what that inheritance means. We will take a short journey through the Bible to look at the big picture from the Garden of Eden to Eternity.

In the Beginning

Inheritance was on God's heart when He created us and the world we live in. In the beginning, the Garden of Eden had a river. (Gen 2:10-14). This river watered the garden, bringing life to everything it touched. It represents the original inheritance, a life of purpose and provision in the presence of God.

God created His people out of love, desiring a relationship

with those who would love Him freely. He gave them the gift of choice, the freedom to follow Him or to turn away. Made in His image, humanity was created to feel, to love and to choose. Yet Adam and Eve, the first people He created, chose disobedience and sin entered the world, bringing a separation between man and God. But God in His sovereignty had a plan.

From Wilderness to Inheritance

Turning to the book of Joshua, we see that God's love for His people, Israel, had not changed. In this Old Testament account, God fulfils His promise of a land prepared for them, a land described as flowing with milk and honey. This inheritance was a sign of His faithfulness and His plans for their future. Their journey into that promise began at the Jordan River. After years of wandering in the wilderness, God led them into the land He had set apart for them.

We read about the miraculous crossing of the Jordan River. As the Israelites stepped into the waters, Scripture says:

> ...the waters which came down from upstream stood still...and all of Israel crossed over on dry ground, until all the people had crossed completely over the Jordan.
>
> Josh 3:16-17 NKJV

After crossing, the Israelites gathered twelve stones from the middle of the river, as God had instructed and set them up at their campsite (Josh 4:3). These stones were meant to serve as a lasting reminder for future generations. To enter the land God had promised, they witnessed His miracle firsthand. God's instruction was clear:

> ...In the future, your children will ask you, **'What do these stones mean?'** Then you can tell them, 'They remind us that the Jordan River stopped flowing when the Ark of the Lord's Covenant went across.' **These stones will stand as a memorial** among the people of Israel forever.
>
> Josh 4:6-7 NLT

These stones were a reminder of God's power, provision and guidance. By remembering what God had done, the Israelites and the generations that followed would be encouraged to trust Him in the future. Crossing the Jordan was about stepping into the inheritance God had prepared for them.

As I read the book of Joshua, I was also struck by the bold, courageous women who stood for their inheritance. Achsah is one such woman who asked her father for water to nourish the land she had received (Josh 15:19). Her request was answered with both upper and lower **springs**, painting a picture of living water that refreshes dry ground and of fruitfulness.

In Joshua 13:7, God instructs Joshua to divide the land as an inheritance. The Old Testament was originally written in Hebrew. Understanding the word used for 'inheritance' deepens our insight into God's intention. The Hebrew term *'nachalah'* conveys 'inheritance, possession, portion, heritage, heirloom or estate.' [1] Even more beautifully, its root, *'nachal'*, means a 'brook, river, stream or a valley through which a stream runs.' [2] Like a spring carrying water, inheritance flows from one generation to the next!

What did David say?

David, who wrote much of the book of Psalms, reflects deeply on the meaning of inheritance. He declares:

> Lord, you alone are my inheritance, my cup of blessing. You guard all that is mine. The land you have given me is a pleasant land. What a wonderful inheritance!
>
> Psalm 16:5-6 NLT

What a beautiful revelation of God's heart towards His people. David was declaring the Lord Himself as his inheritance and his portion. He knew what it meant to inherit the precious presence and provision of God.

Lineage of Grace

Turning to the New Testament, the book of Matthew reveals the stories of five women: Tamar, Rahab, Ruth, Bathsheba and Mary, who are woven into the very genealogy of Jesus. Many of them were Gentiles, outsiders, scandalised or marginalised, which is why their stories are so significant. They were not forgotten! Through their lives, we see a powerful picture of inheritance and grace being passed down, ultimately fulfilled in Christ.

JESUS! Our Inheritance

Because of the fall, humanity was separated from God and what was lost in Eden could not be restored by human effort. But through the cross, Jesus made a way. His sacrifice redeemed us, restoring not only our access to God's inheritance but also our identity as His treasured possession.

In the New Testament, inheritance is about belonging to the family of God through Christ. He brought us into an eternal inheritance, not based on status, race or reputation, but entirely by grace.

It is like a will: when the one who holds the promise passes it on, the beneficiary receives everything that was promised. Jesus died so that we might inherit all He has for us: forgiveness, healing, wholeness, belonging, love, righteousness, eternal life and so much more.

In the New Testament, it is a Person, Jesus Christ Himself, through whom we become heirs of a kingdom that cannot be shaken.

Paul reminds us in his letters to the early churches, that 'In Him also we have obtained an inheritance...' (Eph 1:11 NKJV) and that,

> ...He has enabled you to share in the inheritance that belongs to his people, who live in the light.
>
> Col 1:12 NLT

This inheritance is not earned but freely given. It reminds us that God's plan is perfect and that we are called to live as His children.

Future Inheritance

From the garden of Eden to the gates of eternity, the story of inheritance is God's invitation to belong to Him, to walk with Him, to reign with Him and to be called His own. This journey begins and ends with a river. In the closing pages of Revelation 22:1-2 NIV, we read:

> Then the angel showed me the river of the water of life, as clear as crystal, flowing from the throne of God and of the Lamb down the middle of the great street of the city. On each side of the river stood the tree of life, bearing twelve crops of fruit, yielding its fruit every month. And the leaves of the tree are for the healing of the nations.

Even as we reflect on these promises, we only catch a glimpse of the glory that awaits us. Paul reminds us that our present troubles are temporary, yet there is an eternal home awaiting us, that will be far greater than anything we can imagine in this life (2 Cor 4:17 NIV). Our inheritance is both now and in the future. Our ultimate destination is to live with Him forever. Heaven, our true home, is a place of indescribable beauty, perfect peace and everlasting joy.

Reflecting on this future, I recall how, as a child, I used to imagine the place that Jesus was preparing for me (John 14:2-3). When I couldn't sleep, I pictured heaven instead of counting sheep. I saw beautiful wildflowers and 'smelled' their fragrance filling the air. Jesus is at the centre, in all of His majesty.

This is a place where He will wipe away every tear. Death, sorrow and pain will vanish. We will live in His light, worshipping Him forever (Rev 21:4).

Our true inheritance isn't earthly wealth, but Jesus. It is living forever in God's presence, in the home He prepares for us, where every heart is healed and whole. This is the treasure we long for! This hope shapes us and leads us to live for Him with eternity in our hearts.

> ...To the thirsty I will give water without cost
> from the spring of the water of life.
> Those who are victorious will inherit all this, and
> I will be their God and they will be my children.
>
> Rev 21:6-7 NIV

What a glorious inheritance awaits us!

But what does this mean for us today?

Inheritance received by Grace!

We don't have to earn it; it is freely given! The Israelites did not earn the Promised Land by their perfection, but they received it by God's promise and mercy. At times, we may need to put on our spiritual armour to press into what He has for us, but we can believe in faith that it is ours and we can rest in the knowledge that God has an inheritance for us today! It is entirely the work of His grace!

Springs

Like the springs that Achsah received, these blessings now flow within our hearts, reviving dreams and restoring what was lost. Springs symbolise the life Jesus gives us, refreshing our souls, washing us and satisfying the deepest thirst within us. What the world offers may seem enticing, but it cannot quench the soul. Only Jesus fills our hearts with His peace, joy and abundant life. He alone provides the living water that restores and satisfies the emptiness inside.

And Stones...

Stones represent legacy, God's promises and truth passed on from generation to generation. They are reminders that God makes a way where there seems to be none. The Israelites left the wilderness behind and stepped into identity and destiny. These stones were a reminder to the next generation about how God had brought them into His promises. So when the future generations asked, 'What do these stones mean?' there was a testimony to share. Your life is one of those stones. These stories are the stones that remind us of God's faithfulness.

This Book is also about You and Me!

This book is about the women around me now. Quiet warriors of prayer and bold voices for truth. Women who pursued their inheritance by faith. Their lives illustrate spiritual truths about faith and courage.

You are part of a greater plan. You are a woman of inheritance and you have a heavenly Father who is just waiting to fulfil His calling and purpose through your life. It's your story! And it's my story!

This book is my testimony of the goodness and faithfulness of God in my own life and that of my family. My inheritance is found in Him!

Just this week, my mum said something that stirred deep within me:

> The godly inheritance of our family still flows, even when those who carried it are no longer around.

That truth stayed with me. Our inheritance is not buried with the women who came before us. It still flows. It shapes us and prepares the way for those yet to come.

The Word of God reminds us that He is faithful in His promises:

> Your faithfulness continues through all generations...
>
> Ps 119:90 NIV

He is so good and so faithful. As David declares in Psalms 23:6 NLT:

> Surely your goodness and unfailing love will pursue me all the days of my life, and I will live in the house of the Lord forever.

Maybe you don't come from a long line of believers. But your inheritance still flows—for your own children, your friends and your community, just like the Samaritan woman, whose encounter with Jesus caused her to run back and tell her town all about how He had changed her life (Jn 4:39).

Or maybe, if you don't know Jesus, I pray that the testimonies in this book speak to you about how Jesus can meet you in your story, just where you are and bring you into your inheritance. He longs for you to know Him. He wants to have a relationship with you. He loves you so much. As you read these stories, may God speak to your heart and lead you into a place where He becomes your Lord and Saviour too.

These stories are springs and stones. I am one of them. And so are you!

Reflection

Springs

Are there areas in your life that feel dry? Do you need God's living water to refresh, restore and bring fruitfulness to you?

Stones

What testimonies do you want to leave behind as stones, reminders of God's goodness and faithfulness for others or for the next generation?

Chapter 2

Springs in a Dry Land

Achsah

Bold Daughter of Inheritance

Achsah really stood out when I read the book of Joshua. It's only a small story, but it's really powerful in its meaning. Achsah was born into a legacy of fearless faith. Her Hebrew name means 'anklet' or 'adornment' and 'bursting the veil'. [1] Her story is found in Joshua 15:16-19 and Judges 1:12-15. She was a woman adorned with courage and spiritual strength. Achsah was planted firmly in the promises of God and in the example set by her father.

Just as Isaiah 52:7 ESV declares,

> How beautiful upon the mountains are the feet of him who brings good news, who publishes peace, who brings good news of happiness, who publishes salvation, who says to Zion, 'Your God reigns.'

so too, Achsah's bold request brought not only inheritance but also refreshing. Her feet, like those in Isaiah's vision, carried a message of hope. She walked in faith and brought refreshing to a dry place, just like this messenger with good news!

Her father, Caleb, is described as having 'a different spirit' (Num 14:24, NIV). He followed God 'passionately' (MSG) and 'wholeheartedly' (NIV). The result was that God promised to bring him into the land and into his full inheritance. This is recorded in Deuteronomy 1:36 AMP. God says:

> ...he shall see it, and to him and to his children I
> will give the land on which he has walked
> because he has followed the Lord completely
> [and remained true to Him].

What a beautiful key to unlocking inheritance. It has to do with our heart posture towards God. God desires to lift us above our limitations, to raise us up with wings like eagles (Isa 40:31), seating us with Christ in heavenly places (Eph 2:6). He wants us to think differently, too.

At forty years old, Caleb stood apart from the crowd when he spied out the land of Canaan. While others returned with fear-filled reports, he came back with a declaration of faith. Where fear saw giants, Caleb saw opportunity. Fear whispers, 'We seemed like grasshoppers,' a limited, earthly perspective. But faith sees from heaven's view. Faith agrees with God's promises, not human impossibilities.

Caleb led with a vision aligned to God's heart, refusing to be held back by fear. And forty-five years later, at the age of eighty-five, Caleb was still burning with purpose. He boldly declared, 'Give me this mountain!' (Josh 14:12). He did not settle for less than what God had promised. He had tenacious, enduring faith that asks boldly and receives fully. I think this is where Achsah's faith in God was nurtured. From a young age, she saw her father's faith.

Achsah inherited more than land; she received the same spirit of faith. When she was given in marriage to Othniel and granted land, she noticed it's dryness. Instead of focusing on the desert, she remembered God's promises. She went boldly to her father and asked for what was needed:

> 'Give me a blessing; since you have given me land in the South, give me also springs of water.' So he gave her the upper springs and the lower springs.
>
> Josh 15:19 NKJV

This moment is powerful. Achsah understood her needs and wasn't afraid to ask for more. She requested springs of water and received double: the upper springs and lower springs. This shows that true inheritance must be watered to grow. Her focus was on God as provider. He is El Shaddai, more than enough!

Like Achsah, I too have a father full of faith, full of the Word, unwavering in spiritual authority, wisdom and discernment.

I've received an inheritance from my dad and I am so thankful to God! Spiritual authority passed on in humility. Courage to step into my inheritance, to know God and walk in His purposes for my life!

Achsah's story calls us to steward what God gives and not settle. There are springs to pursue; Go after them; ask boldly! God loves to answer our faith-filled hearts.

There is an inheritance for you!

Our Heavenly Father!

Achsah's life is also a picture of prayer, showing us a beautiful pattern for how we come to our Heavenly Father.

Charles Spurgeon, in his sermon, *Achsah's Asking, A Pattern of Prayer*, reminds us that our requests are pleasing to the heart of God.[2] Like Achsah, we are to come with thoughtful, specific prayers, with thanksgiving for what He has already done. She didn't come demanding. She came knowing. She knew her father. She knew what was needed. And she knew how to ask. Achsah came with gratitude, asked with faith and received with abundance.

We, too, are invited to approach our Heavenly Father in the same way. Jesus said,

> Ask, and it will be given to you; seek, and you will find; knock, and the door will be opened to you.
>
> Matt 7:7 NIV

God desires to bless His children abundantly. Matt 6:8 NKJV reminds us,

> ...your Father knows the things you have need of before you ask Him.

What a tender reassurance that He already knows. And yet, like a loving mother or father who delights in the upward gaze of their child, full of trust and expectation, our Heavenly Father loves to hear us ask. It's not because He is unaware, but because He treasures the intimacy of hearing us ask. So hear Him whisper to your heart today, just as He promised in Isaiah 65:24 NLT

> I will answer them before they even call to Me.
> While they are still talking about their needs,
> I will go ahead and answer their prayers.

What a God! So near, so attentive and so willing. You have a Heavenly Father unlike any earthly father. You are the daughter of a loving Father who never fails, is always with you, accepts you and has good plans for you.

Perhaps you've thought of God as someone you turn to only when you need something, and when things don't go as you hoped, you walk away disillusioned. Many people do the same. Even some public figures have said they 'found God', only to turn away when His plans didn't match their own. They've missed the truth that God is good and always has the best in mind for our lives. His plans are far better than ours!

He's our loving Father who delights to answer when we seek Him.

Today, take a step toward your inheritance. Don't settle for a dry life. God invites you to pursue the spring found only in Him. He is the only One who can satisfy your soul's longing. Trust Him today.

You may not have heard of these words before, but allow them to stir faith in your heart.

Our God is:
Omnipotent – All-powerful.
Omniscient – All-knowing.
Omnipresent – Everywhere at all times.

He is Jehovah-Jireh, our Provider.
Jehovah-Shalom, our Peace.
Jehovah-Raah, our Shepherd.
Jehovah-Rapha, our Healer.
Jehovah Shammah, The Lord is There.
El Roi, the God who sees us.

You can call Him Abba! *'Abba'* is the Aramaic word that means 'Father (and) combines warmth with honour'. [3] It's not irreverent or casual; it's deeply intimate. It reflects the tender way God the Father loves you, a cry straight from the heart expressing the depth of love, affection and closeness we have with our Heavenly Father.

The Message translation captures it beautifully:

> ...Thus we have been set free to experience our rightful heritage. You can tell for sure that you are now fully adopted as his own children because God sent the Spirit of his Son into our lives crying out, 'Papa! Father!' Doesn't that privilege of intimate conversation with God make it plain that you are not a slave, but a child? And if you are a child, you're also an heir, with complete access to the inheritance.
>
> Gal 4:5-7

There are so many more names for God that show us the true nature of who our Father is. I would encourage you to dig into the Word of God and come to know Him for yourself.

Beyond the veil

Achsah's name also carries another powerful meaning: to 'burst the veil.' [4] It is a prophetic whisper of what Christ would ultimately complete for us when He died on the cross. When Jesus breathed His last, the curtain (also known as the veil) in the temple was torn in two from top to bottom (Matt 27:51), symbolising the removal of our separation with God.

Hebrews 10:19-20 NIV declares,

> Therefore, brothers and sisters, since we have confidence to enter the Most Holy Place by the blood of Jesus, by a new and living way opened for us through the curtain, that is, His body...

Through Him, we can come right into His presence. We are welcomed beyond the veil, into the very throne room of God. Achsah's bold approach to her father, asking for more, is a picture of the boldness we now carry as daughters of the King. Her name reminds us that we have total access to God, through Christ and our requests, made in faith, are not only heard but are a delight to the heart of God.

Before Jesus came and made a way for us, only the high priest was allowed to enter the Holy of Holies, the innermost part of the temple where God's presence rested. This priest could enter only once a year to offer a sacrifice on behalf of the people (Heb 9:7). A thick veil separated this holy place, symbolising the barrier between a holy God and sinful humanity. But now, through Jesus, our Great High Priest (Heb 4:14), that barrier has been torn. He offered His own body as the perfect sacrifice for our sins, once and for all (Heb 10:10). It is because of His finished work on the cross that we are invited to come boldly into God's presence, into intimate fellowship with our Father. Through His sacrifice, we have been made holy.

Achsah's story is a call to us to walk in our inheritance. Recognise what we've been given. Don't be afraid to ask your

Father and don't be surprised when He gives you more than you imagined. Ask for eyes of faith to see what God has in store!

Because our Father is still in the business of pouring out the upper and lower springs. The God who gave springs to Achsah is still giving water today.

You are a woman of inheritance!

Reflection

What are you asking your Heavenly Father for right now? Ask Him to place His desires in your heart!

Are you asking boldly? In faith? Know that God has made a way into His presence for you!

Look into the names of God and allow them to stir faith in your heart today.

Chapter 3

Courage to Speak Up!
Daughters of Zelophehad

Bold Women of Inheritance

The other women mentioned in the book of Joshua are the daughters of Zelophehad, who stepped forward to claim their inheritance. Their story begins in Numbers 27:1-11, where they approach Moses after the death of their father, Zelophehad, the grandson of Gilead. With no sons to inherit, these five sisters, Mahlah, Noah, Hoglah, Milcah and Tirzah, stood boldly before Moses and the leaders of Israel, asking that their family line not be forgotten simply because they were daughters. They reminded Moses of God's justice and the Lord answered their request, commanding that if a man died without sons, his inheritance would pass to his daughters. What incredible courage and faith they had! They didn't rebel or demand, but they approached with boldness and wisdom, with a balance between 'a spirit of confrontation and a spirit of cooperation'. [1]

The daughters of Zelophehad didn't only fight for their own inheritance, they reshaped the laws of a nation. Their faith didn't just open doors for themselves, it opened a pathway for generations of women to come. God even ensured the land stayed within their tribal boundaries by giving an additional instruction to marry within their tribe (Num 36), so that no portion of land would be lost from their family.

So when their father died with no sons, their rightful inheritance was at risk. The daughters didn't shrink back. They stepped forward in faith, declaring,

> ...Give to us a possession among our father's brothers.
>
> Num 27:4 ESV

And God answered.

Their story is not only one of justice, it is one of spiritual boldness, fighting to secure what had already been promised. They stood in the confidence of their lineage and claimed their land, not just for themselves, but for the generations to come.

These five daughters were more than names in a list. They were women of strength, unity and prophetic purpose. Each brought something unique to the group. Their personalities, reflected in the meanings of their names, reveal a strong, powerful sisterhood of purpose! Imagine being a fly on the wall as these sisters discussed how they would ask for their inheritance.

'*Noah*' was the calm within the storm. Her name means 'rest' or 'movement' [2] and she carried a quiet confidence, resting in the knowledge that God had already given them a promise. She didn't need to strive, but she knew the land was theirs. She was cool, calm and collected, reminding her sisters to rest in their inheritance, but was also ready to move when God said it was time.

I think Noah would have had a calming effect on '*Hoglah*', whose name means 'partridge' or 'boxer'. [3] She was the fighter; tenacious, outspoken, determined and unwilling to be dismissed. She had the boldness to declare their rights, the kind of woman who wouldn't let fear silence the truth that she knew. She would make sure they were heard! Perhaps she sometimes lacked the wisdom to know when to speak.

This is where '*Milcah*' was needed, the 'queen' or 'counsel', the wise advocate, the one with grace and insight. [4] You can imagine her as the peacemaker, reminding them, 'We are daughters of promise. We belong.'

At times their discussions may have become tense, but thankfully one of the daughters was named '*Tirzah*' meaning 'pleasantness'. [5] She brought encouragement, joy and strength to the group with her warmth and kindness. She was the one they wanted near when they felt tired or discouraged. Her very presence and her heart full of faith lifted the atmosphere and spurred them on. Tirzah knew that justice done with joy is God's delight.

Then we can't forget '*Mahlah*' whose name means 'sickness', who perhaps carried the scars of generational limitation or personal struggle. [6] But she had had enough; she wanted to see an end to what had held her family back. She longed for healing, not just for herself, but for the name of her father, for her future children and for every woman who would come after. Her voice was desperate! She was determined to change her future.

These beautiful sisters knew that God had something better and they were determined to stand for what was rightfully theirs. Together, they stood before Moses and the leaders of Israel, not with entitlement, but with faithful insistence. Each brought her own strength, her own story and her own fire. And God heard them.

> The daughters of Zelophehad speak what is right...
>
> Num 27:7 NKJV

The daughters of Zelophehad are mentioned five times in Scripture, marking the importance of women who rise together to claim what is rightfully theirs in God and in four of those passages, all five names are listed.

The number five in Scripture often symbolises grace, favour and God's goodness. The fact that five daughters stood together, united in purpose, petitioning for inheritance, is deeply prophetic. They were not just asking for land, but contending for grace to be made visible in justice.

These women changed the law for future generations, showing that women are named and heard.

When we hear about them again in Joshua 17:3-6, they stand once more, this time before Eleazar the priest, Joshua and the leaders, to claim what had been promised. These women had a vision for what belonged to them. They trusted in God's provision.

Sometimes God makes a promise, but in faith, we need to see it through by standing on what God has said is ours. Hebrews 11:1 in the Amplified says:

> Now faith is the assurance (title deed, confirmation) of things hoped for (divinely guaranteed), and the evidence of things not seen [the conviction of their reality—faith comprehends as fact what cannot be experienced by the physical senses].

We can have security in God's promises and know that, in His time, they will be fulfilled.

Double Portion Daughters

The daughters of Zelophehad were not just preserving a name; they were also defending their right to a double portion. They were of the tribe of Manasseh, son of Joseph, who had been uniquely blessed. In Genesis 48, Jacob blessed Joseph's two sons, Ephraim and Manasseh, giving each of them a full tribal inheritance. In doing so, Jacob gave Joseph the double portion normally reserved for the firstborn, Reuben. Reuben had forfeited his rights to the double portion inheritance and his inheritance was transferred to the sons of Joseph (1 Chr 5:1).

The Pattern of Double

This theme echoes across Scripture:

> Tamar, through pain and injustice, bore twins, Perez and Zerah. Perez was the one who was found in the very lineage of Christ. Where the world saw scandal, God produced double fruitfulness. We will talk about Tamar later on!

> Elisha asked Elijah for a double portion of his spirit and received it (2 Ki 2:9), performing twice as many recorded miracles.

> Job, after suffering, received double what he had before. (Job 42:10).

And then there is the multiplication beyond double:

> Isaac sowed in famine and reaped a hundredfold (Gen 26:12).

> Deuteronomy 1:11 NIV promises 'May the Lord...increase you a thousand times and bless you as he promised!'

God is not just the God of enough; He is the God of more than enough.

A Personal Reflection

My mother is a twin. It speaks of multiplication and destiny.

Then there is also my sister, Sarah and her husband, Peter, who waited six years with faith and patience to adopt twins from the Philippines. These twins are a promise and an inheritance from God. At the beginning of that long season of hope and preparation, the beautiful boys God had chosen for them, Joel and Daniel, had not yet been born. But God saw them before the foundation of the world (Eph 1:4). He knew their names. He had already written their story. And in the fullness of time, He brought them into a family prepared just for them. It's a picture of God's redemptive heart: patiently contending in love, waiting for the right moment to bring us into our inheritance. Just as the daughters of Zelophehad contended for justice, Sarah and Peter contended in love and heaven responded.

They brought them home when they were just two years old. What a gift they are to us, a living testimony of how God places the lonely in families (Ps 68:6), how He redeems, restores and multiplies through love. These children joined our family and stepped into a legacy. A legacy of faith, inheritance and double blessing. God is still writing stories like those of the daughters of Zelophehad and sometimes, He writes them right into our own homes.

Maybe that's why this story of the daughters grips my heart so strongly. It reminds me that inheritance must be contended for, not through striving, but with faith-filled boldness. The promise may be there, but sometimes we must ask, as these women did and declare, 'This is ours by right.' And when we do, God responds.

Reflection

Are there areas where you need to speak up or step forward in faith to claim your spiritual inheritance?

Is there a double portion that God has been writing into your own story, perhaps in ways you didn't expect?

Part 2
Encounters at a Well

Chapter 4

The God who Sees

Hagar

Today I want to focus on two women: Hagar and the unnamed Samaritan woman. Both experienced profound encounters at the well of Life! Hagar, at her lowest on two separate occasions, found hope and transformation when Jesus met her there!

The First Well

I will take you on the journey of Hagar, a woman who suffered deep injustice at the hands of Sarai, Abram's wife. I feel sorry for Hagar because she didn't choose this story, but was caught up in the decisions others had made for her. In Genesis 16:2 NIV, Sarai said to Abram:

> ...The Lord has kept me from having children. Go, sleep with my slave; perhaps I can build a family through her.

Abram listened and caved in to Sarai's request. In his desire to please Sarai, he took matters into his own hands. Ultimately, it caused a great deal of heartache in his family and his home when Hagar became pregnant. Everything changed and,

> ...When she knew she was pregnant, she began to despise her mistress. Then Sarai said to Abram, 'You are responsible for the wrong I am suffering. I put my slave in your arms, and now that she knows she is pregnant, she despises me...'
>
> Gen 16:4-5 NIV

Caught in a dysfunctional household, Abram stepped back from the conflict and said to Sarai;

> Your slave is in your hands... do with her whatever you think best.
>
> Gen 16:6 NIV

It's not hard to imagine the jealousy and pain brewing in Sarai's heart, even though this was her own idea. And it's easy to feel compassion for Abram, perhaps unsure of how to manage his divided family. What a messy situation they were in.

But in the midst of it all was Hagar, looked down upon, mistreated,and used.

Sarai, overwhelmed by her own grief and longing,

> ...dealt harshly with her...
>
> Gen 16:6 NKJV

So Hagar fled, pregnant, alone and rejected into the wilderness. We often talk about how God meets us at our lowest. Hagar is the first person in Scripture to experience that kind of divine encounter in such a vulnerable moment.

> The angel of the Lord found Hagar near a spring in the desert... and he said, 'Hagar, slave of Sarai, where have you come from, and where are you going?'
>
> Gen 16:7-8 NIV

Notice the question. The angel calls her by name, Hagar. He knows who she is and what she's running from. Hagar answers honestly:

> ...I'm running away from my mistress Sarai...
>
> 16:8 NIV

The angel then tells her to return and submit, but not without declaring a powerful promise over her child. He tells her to name the boy Ishmael, meaning:

> ...(God hears), Because the Lord has heard and paid attention to your persecution (suffering).
>
> Gen 16:11 AMP

In that desert place, by that spring of water, Hagar encounters something no one else in Scripture has yet expressed in such a personal way. She declares:

> 'You are the God who <u>sees</u> me,' for she said, 'I have now seen the One who <u>sees</u> me.'
>
> Gen 16:13 NIV

The Hebrew name she uses is *'El Roi'*; *'El'* meaning 'God' and *'Roi'* meaning 'seeing'[1].

This was not a distant God she met, but He was near — a God who perceived her pain and understood her suffering. The Amplified expands on this verse:

> ...after seeing Him [who sees me with understanding and compassion]?

and another version, the ESV says:

> ...Truly here I have seen him who looks after me.

Being seen by God means more than a momentary encounter; it's a deep recognition of our struggles and needs. God sees you fully, meets you in your pain and offers hope, showing He is near even when you feel invisible.

In yet another version, Hagar says:

> ...Or have I here also seen [the future purposes or designs of] Him Who sees me?
>
> Gen 16:13 AMPC

I believe in that moment of time, hope arose in her heart for the purposes for which God had for her life. Today, I pray that God's plans for your life will come alive as you come to the well of the One who sees you and not only sees you but loves you intently and has a good future for you.

It is from this moment that the name of the well is given: Beer Lahai Roi, which means:

> ...well of the Living One who sees me.
>
> Gen 16:14 NLT

It's the first recorded moment of a person naming God in such an intimate way. [2] A woman, alone in the wilderness, rejected by people, but not by God.

The Second Well – God Opens Her Eyes

The story of Hagar does not end in Genesis 16. In Genesis 21, we see her again, this time with her son Ishmael. She had returned to Sarai, but the pain hadn't disappeared. If anything, it has deepened.

Note to reader:
Between Genesis 16 and Genesis 21, God changed Abram's name to Abraham, and Sarai's name to Sarah. In the earlier part of Hagar's story, they are referred to as Abram and Sarai. By the time of Genesis 21, they are referred to as Abraham and Sarah, names that reflect God's covenant promise and unfolding plan.

Sarah still couldn't bear the sight of Hagar and the boy. Perhaps the presence of Ishmael was a constant reminder of the impatience and brokenness that filled their home and:

> ...Sarah saw the son whom Hagar the Egyptian had borne to Abraham was mocking, and she said to Abraham, 'Get rid of that slave woman and her son for that woman's son will never share in the inheritance with my son Isaac.'
>
> Gen 21:9-10 NIV

Abraham was deeply distressed. Ishmael was his son, too. But God, in His sovereignty, told Abraham to listen to Sarah, assuring him that Ishmael would not be forgotten.

So once again, Hagar was sent away. This time she was holding her child's hand. Abraham gave her some bread and a skin of water and sent her off into the wilderness of Beersheba. No shelter. No map. Barely surviving.

Eventually, the water ran out. And so did her hope.

> When the water in the skin was gone, she put the boy under one of the bushes. Then she went off and sat down about a bowshot away, for she thought, 'I cannot watch the boy die.' And as she sat there, she began to sob.
>
> Gen 21:15-16 NIV

Can you imagine the heartbreak? This wasn't just physical exhaustion; it was deep soul anguish. A mother who had done everything asked of her now watches her child perish in the wilderness.

But,

> God heard the boy crying, and the angel of God called to Hagar from heaven and said to her, 'What is the matter, Hagar? Do not be afraid; God has heard the boy crying as he lies there.

> Lift the boy up and take him by the hand, for I will make him into a great nation.'
>
> Gen 21:17-18 NIV

Once again, God met Hagar in her wilderness. He reminded her not to fear. He reaffirmed the promise.

And then something beautiful happened.

> ...God opened her eyes and she saw a well of water...
>
> Gen 21:19 NIV

The well had been there all along. In her grief, Hagar couldn't see it. She filled the skin with water and gave her son a drink. God had preserved them again. And from that moment on, we are told:

> God was with the boy as he grew up. He lived in the desert and became an archer.
>
> Gen 21:20 NIV

Hagar's story is one of repeated rejection. Twice she was cast into the wilderness. Twice she met God. Twice she was seen, heard and given a promise.

This second well is a powerful picture of God's sustaining grace. When all hope seems lost, God opens our eyes. He shows us the well of provision we didn't know was there.

The name of this well is not recorded in Genesis 16, but the encounter was a moment of divine rescue. A moment where heaven bends low to meet a mother's broken heart.

If you feel lost and exhausted, there is hope. God sees you. God hears your cry and He will not abandon you. Ask Him to open your eyes to see the Well. His name is Jesus.

The well where He found Hagar still speaks today. It's a stone in the wilderness, a reminder of a God who sees and hears. This story encourages us that His presence brings hope, even in our hardest moments.

Deep Cries to Deep

There's a kind of cry that goes beyond words. It's the cry of a soul unravelling in the wilderness. It's the sound of a mother weeping as she lays her child down under a bush. It's the ache of abandonment, the silent scream of injustice. It's the voice that trembles not from fear but from exhaustion, when there is simply nothing left to give.

This was Hagar's cry. And in that moment, deep cried unto deep. The psalmist echoes her cry in Psalm 42:7 NIV:

> Deep calls to deep in the roar of your waterfalls;
> all your waves and breakers have swept over me.

The depth of Hagar's suffering called out to the depths of God's mercy. The wells were not just sources of water, but encounters with the Source of Life.

Hagar's story is the story of a real woman. In the midst of her troubles, God saw her and met her in her desperation.

And He gave her a name to hold onto when her world fell apart: El Roi –'The God Who Sees Me.'

Reflection

When you reflect on Hagar's wilderness moments, what is God asking you to see differently in your own life or circumstances?

Where have you experienced God's justice at work in your own story?

How might God use your story to bring hope and healing to others who feel unseen or forgotten?

Chapter 5

Encounter at the Well
The Samaritan Woman

Hundreds of years after Hagar's encounter at the well, another woman comes to draw water in the heat of the day at a different well named Jacob's Well. We can read this story in John 4. It is more than a meeting between Jesus and an outcast woman. It is a moment that reveals God's desire to restore what is broken and bring true fulfilment where there has been rejection. This woman was a Samaritan of mixed race, part Jew and part Gentile. Samaritans were rejected by the Jews because they could not prove their genealogy. [1]

Long before the Samaritan woman stood beside this well, God told a striking parable through the prophet Ezekiel about two sisters (Ez 23). These sisters had been chosen by God, set apart as His own, yet they gave themselves over to false lovers, nations and idols that seduced and oppressed them. These sisters pursued fulfilment outside of the One who loved them. Their hearts were divided and they reaped the consequences of choosing other gods. It shows us the deep human tendency to seek satisfaction in the wrong places, to try to quench our souls' thirst from polluted wells. Even their names are significant and give an interesting take on the story of the Samaritan woman at the well.

'*Oholah*' means 'her tent' and represented Samaria, the capital of Israel, a people who chose their own way of worship. '*Oholibah*' means 'My tent is in her' and represented Jerusalem, the capital of Judah, implying true worship of God was to be in Jerusalem.' [2]

Jesus Rewrites the Story

Where Israel failed and where Samaria wandered, Jesus stepped in and rewrote the story, one woman at a time. He didn't come to condemn. He came to redeem.

This reveals the very heart of God. From the beginning, His desire was to be with His people. He longed to place His presence, not beside them, but within them.

We see in the story of the Samaritan woman that Jesus wanted to reveal something deeper about Himself and what He came to do.

In John 4, Jesus walks into Samaria, the land of *Oholah*, the sister who represented 'her own tent', and meets a woman who, like her own people, had searched for love in all the wrong places.

But instead of condemnation, Jesus offers her an invitation. Not to religion or tradition, but to Living Water. She came to the well to draw water, but left with a spring of life inside her.

Jesus was a Jew, she a Samaritan, two groups divided by history, religion and bitterness.

He was a man, she a woman, a radical moment in a culture that frowned upon such interactions.

She had an earthly thirst, but Jesus pointed to a greater thirst, one not satisfied by any well dug into the ground, but by the Living Water only He could give.

> ...whoever drinks of this water will thirst again, but whoever drinks of the water that I shall give him will never thirst. But the water that I shall give him will become in him a fountain of water springing up into everlasting life.
>
> John 4:13-14 NKJV

Then, in this encounter, she asked Jesus whether they should worship on this mountain (Mount Gerizim, where Samaritans worshipped) or in Jerusalem (where Jews insisted it must take place). For generations, these debates have divided people.

But Jesus gently shifted the focus:

> ...a time is coming and has now come when the true worshippers will worship the Father in the spirit and in truth, for they are the kind of

> worshipers the Father seeks. God is Spirit, and His worshipers must worship in the Spirit and in truth.
>
> John 4:23-24 NIV

Just like Oholibah's name suggested, 'My tent is in her', this is what Jesus was revealing: that true worship was no longer about a mountain or a temple, but about the heart. It is about people who would become the new tent, the living temple where God's Spirit would dwell.

The New Temple

In that moment, Jesus introduced a new kind of worship, not bound by a place, but flowing from the heart. The woman, marked by shame and hiding in the heat of the day, was the first in Scripture to hear that God is Spirit and that worship is no longer confined to a mountain or a temple.

Paul later echoes this truth when he writes:

> Do you not know that your bodies are temples of the Holy Spirit, who is in you, whom you have received from God?...
>
> 1 Cor 6:19 NIV

The old tabernacle was a tent of meeting. But now, in Christ, we are His tent and His Spirit lives in us. We don't worship from the outside in, we worship from the inside out.

Jesus reached into her story with a prophetic word that unlocked her future. He told her the truth about her life, not to shame her, but to call her higher. And in doing so, He released her into her destiny. The woman who once hid from her town became a voice in it:

> Come, see a man who told me everything I ever did. Could this be the Messiah?
>
> John 4:29 NIV

The Seventh Man – Wholeness at the Well

At this well, Jesus gently revealed to the Samaritan woman something no one else would have known unless they were God:

> ...you have had five husbands, and the man you now have is not your husband. What you have said is quite true.
>
> John 4:18 NIV

It wasn't just a statement, but it was a prophetic unlocking of her heart that day.

This woman had been through six relationships. Whether through rejection, death, divorce or survival, we don't know the details. What we do know is that by the time she came to that well, her heart was worn, bruised and empty. She had gone from man to man, trying to fill her heart with love. But every time, she came up dry.

And then Jesus came. The seventh man. The Messiah.

The number seven in Scripture often represents completion, wholeness and restoration. On the seventh day, God rested because His work was finished (Gen 2:2-3). In the seventh man, this woman found the rest and completion that her soul had longed for. Jesus didn't come to expose her or to shame her, but He came to reveal Himself so He could restore her.

Her broken story found its completion in Him.

She came to the well empty. She left overflowing. She came alone. She left with a voice. She came out of hiding and began to testify.

Jesus, the seventh man, didn't just know her past, but He offered her a new future.

The God who saw Hagar in the desert is the same God who saw this woman in Samaria. And He is the same God who sees you.

This Living Water, Jesus Himself, is the answer to every soul's cry. He meets us in the wilderness. He opens our eyes to wells we never saw. He doesn't just hand us water. He is our well!

These stories declare a deeper truth:

You are seen. You are heard. You are known. You are loved.

Let the depths of your heart cry out to Him today. He will meet you with Living Water. And that water will become a spring!

Reflection

In what areas of your life are you ready to drink deeply from the well that never runs dry? How can Jesus, the Living Water, refresh and complete you today?

Has a prophetic word or a specific verse ever shifted the course of your life like Jesus' words did for the Samaritan woman?

What word is God speaking over you right now?

Part 3
Daughters of Today

Chapter 6

Simple Faith

Judith

Just like Hagar in the wilderness and the Samaritan woman at the well, there are women today who have encountered the same Living Water. Women who have cried out from dry and desperate places and have been met by the God who sees, hears and restores. Their stories are supernatural, powerful testimonies of the Living God whom we serve.

This story is about one such woman, a beautiful friend named Judith. In her time of great need, she discovered Jesus, the true Well. Her journey is a modern testimony that reveals just how good God is and the power of His grace radiates through her life. Jesus reached into her darkness and brought her into His Kingdom of Light.

Judith was already seventy-one years old when she first heard the message of Jesus. She knew of Jesus only by name, but no one had ever told her about Him before. When she heard the truth of the Gospel, her heart came alive. She believed. She trusted. She followed.

Once immersed in witchcraft and paganism, she was drawn by the gentle call of Jesus. When He came knocking, she didn't hesitate. She opened her heart and never looked back.

Her husband, B.J, shared the gospel with her after recently returning to faith himself. Previously, he had practised Shamanism before experiencing the overwhelming love of God. He wanted to share this good news and decided to tell Judith about Jesus. She accepted Jesus into her heart, too!

For Judith, encountering the truth of Jesus meant simply believing. Her heart became a home for Christ and her life was filled with peace. Her faith was simple; she came to Jesus like a child with a heart of acceptance, saying yes to everything He had for her. She had tasted every kind of spiritual counterfeit, but she finally realised what she had been searching for all along and her heart responded in thankfulness.

A Home for Her Heart

Her story is one of freedom and steadfastness. Though her past was full of spiritual searching, once she found the Truth, she never looked back. She stood firm and her life became a witness to the power of the true Gospel and the deep rest that comes from knowing you're home.

She was delivered from deception, as God's peace and joy filled her heart. She is a testimony to God's power to save completely. She was unwavering in her trust in God when she surrendered.

The lyrics of an old song, *Give Your Heart a Home* by Don Francisco, resonated strongly within her.[1] This song is an invitation. It's about surrendering the weary, wounded places of your heart to the One who created it.

We spend so much of our lives searching for belonging, healing and peace, but all of those things are found only when Jesus becomes the Lord of our lives and the centre of everything we are and do. He's not asking for perfection. He's simply asking to come in. When we open the door of our heart to Him, He brings security, peace, love and His overwhelming presence and He promises that He will never leave us. This is where healing begins!

With an open heart, she received forgiveness from the Lover of her soul, the only One who could fill the empty void within. For years, she had sought to fill her heart with that which couldn't satisfy, but when she encountered Jesus, she came to know the reality of a God who loved her and wanted a relationship with her.

Waters of Obedience

As she trusted God, she took obedient steps in her journey of faith. She followed Him into the waters of baptism. Just as the Israelites crossed the Jordan into the promised land, she left her old life behind and embraced her new life in Christ.

Baptism marked her decision to follow Jesus wholeheartedly. It was an outward sign of an inward transformation of her faith and trust in Christ.

In the waters of baptism, something beautiful happened. As she surrendered her old life and rose into the new, she also received a precious gift, her heavenly prayer language. This is a spiritual language, often called speaking in tongues, where a person is enabled by the Holy Spirit to pray beyond their natural understanding. It's not learned or taught, it's a personal and intimate way of connecting with God, spirit to Spirit.

The struggle was over when she gave up her old life and surrendered to God.

In Ephesians 3:17-18 NLT, Paul prays:

> Then Christ will make his home in your hearts as you trust in him. Your roots will grow down into God's love and keep you strong. And may you have the power to understand, as all God's people should, how wide, how long, how high and how deep His love is.

When Christ makes His home in our hearts, we no longer need to strive to belong. This is your inheritance – if you are tired or weary, come home!

Whether it's your first time, like Judith, or returning home, like BJ, the invitation is the same: come to Him and He will satisfy your soul. The same God who rescued Judith and BJ from darkness and sin, wrapped his arms of love around them and brought them home, is ready to meet you, too.

Judith's inheritance is not complicated. It's not wrapped in religious performance. It is simple, Jesus made a home in her heart and she let Him in.

That is her testimony and that is her inheritance. Isaiah, the prophet, describes the true Well,

> Joyfully you'll pull up buckets of water from the wells of salvation. And as you do it, you'll say, 'Give thanks to God...'
>
> Isa 12:3 MSG

Reflection

I want to ask two questions today;

Do you know Jesus? Is your heart open to invite Him in and allow Him to be the Lord of your life?

Have you wandered, but today you hear God gently calling you back to His love and back into a relationship with Him? He's there waiting with open arms.

Chapter 7

Free Indeed

Felicity Jayne

Invitation to His Promises

Like Judith, Felicity is another dear friend with whom I share life. Both of these precious women continue to teach me so much and the friendship we share is something I deeply cherish.

Felicity's life and writing have deeply inspired me. Her book *Free Indeed: Finding True Joy* [1] stirred something in me and little did I know that I would soon find myself writing a book of my own. Alongside Felicity's story, my mum's and my grandma's stories have also been a source of inspiration as I sat down to write this book.

Felicity helped me believe this book I am writing was possible. She encouraged me not to overthink it, but to simply sit and allow the Holy Spirit to flow through the words. And that's what I'm doing now.

Her story is powerful. In *Free Indeed*, Felicity writes with raw honesty about a season where she felt crushed under a weight of shame. She once described it to me as having mud all over her, as if she were buried under something she couldn't wash off. She didn't feel worthy to represent Jesus, as though her reputation was in ruins.

But here's the truth: it wasn't her sin or failure that caused that weight. What she was carrying wasn't even hers. The shame she felt had roots in generational pain and brokenness, things passed down through her family line that tried to destroy and define her. It was a spiritual inheritance of heaviness, not of her choosing, but it threatened to overshadow the truth of who she was in Christ. I remember encouraging her not to allow the enemy to define her life, to rebuke the enemy's voice and to rise up in her inheritance.

And she did. Felicity began to rise in truth once again. She allowed God to speak louder than shame. She began to walk in the authority that was always hers as a daughter of God. Her life continues to be a radiant testimony to Jesus. She shines with grace and beauty. She walks in freedom and she helps others do the same.

Felicity has a way of drawing out purpose in people. She helps others see the value of their spiritual inheritance and encourages them to walk boldly in the freedom for which they were designed. She doesn't just receive her own inheritance; she calls others into theirs. She walks alongside women as they move from wilderness to rest, from shame to strength, from barrenness into life. Through her life and her words, she speaks refreshing and encouraging words that build up other women in their faith.

It's in the living area of her home, overlooking the ocean, that Felicity shares her love for God with other women—calling them into the fullness of their spiritual inheritance. Each month, she prepares a beautiful banquet, not only with food that nourishes the body but also with a feast from the Word that feeds the soul. Her home becomes a sanctuary, her table a place of encounter and her words a gentle invitation into God's promises.

Stones to Keep, Stones to Let Go

I remember a time Felicity shared a powerful illustration with the women gathered in her home.

She passed around a bag filled with stones she had collected from the sea, just a short walk from her house. Each woman was invited to take a stone in her hand. Felicity explained that these stones represent the things that weigh us down, like unforgiveness, disappointment or shame. For the living water to flow, we need to remove the rocks that block our relationship with Him.

With tenderness, she encouraged us to pray together, asking God to reveal what each stone might symbolise in our lives. 'Some stones need to be released,' she said. 'Not every stone is meant to be carried.'

It was a simple act, yet deeply profound. I will never forget the quiet sound of women letting go, both of the stones in their hands and the burdens in their hearts.

Felicity's story is one of resilience, of choosing to live freely and lightly, even when the weight she once carried wasn't hers to bear. Through seasons of trauma and pain, she discovered the deep rest that can only be found in Jesus.

And now, she gently leads others to that same place of peace. She brings them to the Word of God and reminds them that their identity is not shaped by the past, but by what God has already declared over their lives. Felicity would tell you with quiet conviction: finding rest for your soul is your inheritance. And if she found it, you can too.

Jesus said:

> Come to me, all you who are weary and burdened, and I will give you rest. Take my yoke upon you and learn from me, for I am gentle and humble in heart, and you will find rest for your souls. For my yoke is easy and my burden is light.
>
> Matt 11:28-30 NIV

Don't Dwell on the Past

This chapter wouldn't be complete without mentioning Felicity's beautiful mum. Her life, too, is marked by resilience, by a quiet, steadfast faith that has carried her through deep pain, trauma and grief. Amid unanswered questions and the struggle to make sense of what had happened, she chose to trust God completely. Her eyes are set on the future He has for her, not on the past that could have held her back. She carries a powerful testimony that healing begins when we stop rehearsing the pain and start resting in His promises.

One of the keys to your inheritance in God is this: don't dwell on what was, but step into the future He has for you!

> Forget the former things; do not dwell on the past. See, I am doing a new thing! Now it springs up; do you not perceive it? I am making a way in the wilderness and streams in the wasteland. The wild animals honour me, the jackals and the owls, because I provide water in the wilderness and streams in the wasteland, to give drink to my people, my chosen, the people I formed for myself that they may proclaim my praise.
>
> Isa 43:18-21 NIV

Felicity and her mum are beautiful examples of restoration. And to me, they are a living reminder that even when shame runs in the family, inheritance runs deeper and Jesus gets the final word.

When I think about my friend, Flick, her generosity reminds me of the Proverb which says:

> Whoever brings blessing will be enriched, and one who waters will himself be watered.
>
> Prov 11:25 ESV

Reflection

Are you living freely and lightly in Christ, or are you carrying burdens that aren't yours to carry? Are there 'stones' (shame, fear, expectations, past experiences, generational wounds) that you need to hand over to Him today?

Who in your life has encouraged you to walk in your inheritance?

How might you now become that voice of encouragement for someone else?

Chapter 8

Peace in the Valley

Judy

Judy is a woman whose life speaks without shouting. She is my beautiful mother-in-law, but more than that, she is a faithful woman of God who truly deserves to be honoured in this book.

Diagnosed with Parkinson's disease, she has walked through what many would call a dark valley, but she has done it with light in her eyes and peace in her soul. Her strength is not loud, but it is unshakeable. Her legacy is not just in what she has done, but in who she has remained.

There is a peace in her heart that surpasses understanding and Judy lives in it. Her spirit carries a deep calm that is not circumstantial, but eternal. Even in physical weakness, her life overflows with the fruit of the Spirit, especially gentleness and self-control. She does not complain. She does not strive. She simply trusts. Her quiet spring is one of peace, where she lies down to rest in green pastures, knowing she has all that she needs.

Judy is a stone in our family story, a landmark of faith under pressure. She has chosen gratitude over grumbling, and worship over worry. Her illness has not defined her, but she walks in the peace and perseverance given to her by Jesus. She remains constant in the storm.

She is a woman of deep inner stillness, despite physical trial and her life speaks louder than words. She is a model of grace, acceptance and unwavering trust in Jesus and an unspoken witness to the power of joy in suffering.

Even in her suffering, we see how deeply God cared for Judy. One day, while walking in a park with Brian, my father-in-law, Judy had another fall, something that had happened to her before. This time, her lip was split and her tooth was knocked out.

But in God's tender care, help came in an unexpected form. A man, perhaps a dentist or maybe even an angel, stopped to assist. With wisdom and calm, he gently reset the tooth.

Later that day, Judy visited her own dentist, who confirmed that her tooth had been saved. What an amazing miracle! God sees. He surrounds us with His angels, ministering spirits sent to protect and help us when we need them most. It may have been only a man, but the Bible does tell us that we entertain angels unawares. (Heb 13:2) How many times do we encounter angels and not even know it!

Judy's inheritance is not land or riches, but peace in the presence of God. It is a still river flowing through her, a quiet strength passed down to her family, friends and generations yet to come. She reminds us that our true inheritance is found in resting securely in the Father's hands, no matter the outward circumstances.

Judy carries the inheritance of peace and the presence of God. And so can you. This promise is for you today.

> You will keep in perfect peace those whose minds
> are steadfast, because they trust in you.
>
> Isa 26:3 NIV

Reflection

Have you gone through a challenging time when God gave you a sense of calm and peace, even when things didn't make sense? What helped you keep your mind on God during that season?

How can you become more aware of God's quiet provisions, even during suffering or uncertainty?

Part 4
Generational Wells

Chapter 9

Prayer Warrior

Ruth, my Gran

This part of my journey through women's stories is a personal walk through the generations of my own family. It starts with my grandma, Ruth, whose quiet strength and faithfulness laid our spiritual foundation and continues with my mum, Anthea, a woman of prayer and perseverance whose life reflects the love of God.

My story, weaves into theirs, like a thread in a tapestry. I have seen how faith is passed down, not only by words but by example — prayers whispered in the dark and courage shown in the light.

Now I watch as my children walk their own paths, still guided by the prayers that came before them. Already, I see glimpses of the next generation, emerging with their hearts full of promise.

This is more than a family tree. It is a testimony of God's faithfulness, from my Gran, the first prayer warrior, continuing through each generation.

A Legacy of Prayer, Scripture and Generational Grace

In every family of faith, there is someone who becomes the first to dig a well, someone who chooses to trust God when the path is uncertain. For me, that someone was my gran.

Her memoirs, lovingly titled *Ruth's Story*, paint the picture of a courageous, compassionate woman who lived her life for Jesus and loved every moment she was given. She wasn't just faithful in public; she was faithful in the quiet places in prayer, in the Word, as a mother and as a grandmother.

The Prayer of a Mother's Heart

My grandma didn't just hope for a family, she prayed for one. Psalm 128:3 NIV became a promise she clung to:

> Your wife will be like a fruitful vine within your house; your children will be like olive shoots around your table.

She held this Scripture close as she waited and watched God answer her prayers across the decades. This verse shaped her expectations, her prayers and her hope for what God could do through the generations. My mum writes of her:

> The war years and a young husband overseas in the army drove Ruth to a learned trust in the Lord. Psalm 128:3 was earmarked with a

PP (Precious Promise) in her bible in 1940. It was a long time to be married without a family and she held tightly to the truth that she would be a fruitful vine and have children like olive shoots around her table. She loved that verse and throughout her life, she would talk of her olive shoots.

A Woman of the Word

Ruth wrote in the conclusion of her memoirs:

> Now, to sum it up. I feel that God has been very good to me and our family. We have had our ups and downs. Not everything has been plain sailing, but we or should I say I, have learned to trust the Lord for so many things in life. I thank Him for the way He has given me Scriptures...

This closing reflection reveals the heart of a woman anchored in truth. She left more than memories. Her spiritual inheritance in the Word of God became stones of remembrance and hope for the future.

A Flowing Inheritance

When I speak of the flow of generational inheritance, I draw from her life. Her prayers continue to echo. Her faith still speaks and the Scriptures she treasured have shaped our family!

Her story is not finished; it is still being lived out through children, grandchildren and great-grandchildren who carry her love for Jesus.

I feel privileged to have had someone in my life who didn't just tell me about God, but showed me what it meant to walk with Him. My gran was faithful in prayer. Every day, she would lift each of her children and grandchildren before the Lord. One song that captures her legacy is *Talking to Jesus* by Elevation Worship.[1] When I heard it for the first time, I could see her in those lyrics, on her knees in prayer, I could see my mum and I could see me!

She was a quiet warrior, praying, caring, guarding the spiritual soil where my life was planted. I am grateful. Even now, as she has passed on, her legacy flows through me, to my children and theirs.

At the Mention: Peace, Presence, Jesus

I always remember one of her favourite songs that was played at her funeral, a moment I couldn't physically be there for, since she lived in England and I was here in Australia. But I remember listening to that song across the distance, letting the words carry me back into her presence, into her legacy of quiet faith and unwavering prayer.

The song was *Jesus, Just the Mention of Your Name*.[2] Even now, when I listen to it, it's more than a song; it's a reminder of who Jesus is and what His Name brings into the lives of those who call on Him.

The name, Jesus, meant everything to her. It brought life where things seemed barren, warmth and comfort in sorrow, direction in storms and peace amid trials. Jesus' name was bread on empty days and water for a dry soul. This song reminds me that Jesus, who gave her strength, still speaks life into me, my children and future generations.

Jesus. Just the mention of His Name.

By the Fire: The Warmth of His Presence

Right now, I'm sitting in front of our warm fire. The room is still, the flames dance gently and I can't help but think. This warmth, this peace, reminds me of Jesus. It's Him. It's always been Him. The One who brings comfort in the cold, clarity in the storm and life to the deepest parts of our hearts.

Precious daughter, your inheritance is found in Jesus. Not in striving, not in performance, but in Him. He is the Living Water for your soul when life feels empty or dry. He is the fire that melts your heart. He is the Name above every other name, gentle enough to heal, powerful enough to save.

Let Him refresh you today. Let the warmth of His presence soften the hard places. Just speak His name. He hears even the quietest whisper!

The same Jesus who walked with my Gran, who sustained my mum, who rescued and called me, is walking with you now. He is your portion today.

Just the mention of His name... and everything begins to change.

When the Rain Comes: Beauty in the Barren

I'll never forget those rare, extraordinary moments when the rain finally came in Coober Pedy. Our children would race outside with wide eyes and open hearts, laughing as waterfalls tumbled down the sides of our dugout home. The dry, cracked land transformed before our eyes, mud pools became swimming holes, frogs began to croak after long silence, butterflies emerged as if they'd been waiting all along. and wildflowers and Sturt desert peas burst into bloom after years of dormancy.

It was wild. Beautiful. Unexpected. And it spoke to something deep in me.

Jesus is like that rain.

When He comes, when we call on His name, He doesn't always arrive the way we expect, but oh, how He transforms our barren places. He stirs joy where there's been silence. He brings life from what looked forgotten. He causes beauty to rise out of places long left dry and waiting.

This is your inheritance. It may be hidden, but mention His name and He will refresh your soul.

Reflection

How are you intentionally cultivating a prayer life that covers others, your family and the generations to come?

What might God be inviting you to pray over them today?

Are there promises in God's Word that you need to stand on or perhaps ones you've forgotten or let go of?

What verses can you begin to declare over your life and your circumstances right now?

Chapter 10

Language of Love

Anthea, my Mum

My mum means more to me than words can ever truly say. She has been a steady stream of grace in my life, quietly and powerfully shaping the way I see the world and the God who made it. The springs that flow through me today were first stirred by her prayers, her wisdom and her unwavering love.

From her, I have inherited a deep faith, a love for God's Word and a heart for worship. She doesn't just talk about the Lord; she lives it and in doing so, she continues to pass on a living inheritance. Her life is such a beautiful example to me and a picture of the generational flow of inheritance and how, when we surrender our lives to God, a spring is released to future generations.

My mum finds wonder in the world and she sees it everywhere. She is an artist, painting pictures of the natural life around us, but also a digital artist, capturing beauty with grace and intention. In the room where I write now, two of her 'I am' statements about Jesus hang on the wall in front of me. One draws my eyes to 'I am Jesus, the True

Vine' (John 15:5) and the other to the words, 'I am Jesus, the Way, the Truth, and the Life' (John 14:6). Within one of these art works is a picture of the wooden cross that stands in the underground church we previously attended in Coober Pedy. Behind these pictures are faint words that describe our inheritance, such as peace, blessed, sing, dance, celebrate, faith, joy, abundance, love...Her artwork is such an encouragement, not only to me, but to others who have it decorating their walls, too.

She also loves to journal her walk with Jesus. Her expressions stir faith in quiet, powerful ways. One of her books, *Magnify: Short Verse Exalting Creator God*, was written 'to release a new level of faith in the reader and advance His Kingdom.' That is exactly what it does.

When people speak of my mum, their words are wrapped in love. They speak of her gentleness, her kindness and her depth. There's a humility in her that draws people in and a quiet strength that lifts them up. Sometimes I wonder, am I living up to the same legacy of faith and tenderness?

But I am reminded that God calls each of us in His own special way. While my mum's springs of creativity flow through her words and her pictures, mine may pour out differently. And that's okay. We each reflect a part of His nature through the uniqueness of who God created us to be.

She is a woman of faith and her life echoes Paul's words: 'I die daily.' That surrender is not spoken loudly; it's lived. And I hear it even now, not in her words, but in her gentle example.

Love and Light

What continues to stand out to me in my mum's life are her reflections as a young twelve-year-old growing up in Blantyre, Nyasaland (now Malawi). In her book, she shares a memoir titled *Blessings in Blantyre*. Within its pages, she recounts the life of a remarkable missionary who exemplified simple, faithful obedience. Her name is Corrie Ten Boom.

Corrie once stayed with my mum's family and it was an extraordinary moment that left a lasting impact, particularly on my mum. It wasn't just Corrie's presence that mattered; it was the spirit of humility and deep love she carried. That visit became a moment that helped shape a generation.

Corrie had a way of speaking that everyone could understand. Her language was love, spoken not only in her words but in her actions. My mum shared a powerful illustration that still echoes in her heart:

> She pulled out a little torch. We all expected it to shine, but it didn't. She explained the battery was missing. She placed a battery inside, but still, no light came. Then she found a blockage inside. When that was cleared and the power source was connected, the torch shone brightly.
>
> Corrie explained: 'We are like that torch. We need the Holy Spirit as our battery—our source of life and power. But even with the Spirit in us, blockages like unforgiveness, pride or fear

can keep our light from shining. Only when we allow God to clear those away can His love shine through us fully.'

My mum lives that truth. Her life and her art reflect a deep surrender, a willingness to let the Spirit illuminate every part of her. Like Corrie, she has written incredible books and her life is a lamp that lights the path for others, not by striving, but by letting God's love flow freely through her.

This is one of many of her poems, written to show the magnificent beauty of the One we adore:

God of Love

Your love so deep, so undeserved
For fallen man like me,
A tiny spot who you embrace,
A marvellous mystery.

Amazing love that you should die,
On that cruel wooden cross,
So great my God the love you gave,
The price to save the lost,

You hold me close, so very close,
I hear your tender heart,
Your abundant grace, extravagant love,
So deep, so rich and vast.

The love that binds me close, Lord
Your heartbeat that I feel,
Infuse with my own heartbeat,
That your love may flow through me.

Reflection

In what ways is your life reflecting the love of God to those around you?

What does it look like for you to 'magnify the Lord' in your life? How are your words, your work and your worship pointing others to the beauty and greatness of God?

Do you see God as Creator, not just of the world, but of your life, your story and your gifts?

Is your light shining brightly? Ask the Holy Spirit to reveal and gently remove anything that stops His light from shining fully.

Chapter 11

My Story

Rachel

From Grey Skies to New Horizons

I lived in England until I was eleven. I was born in Coventry and spent my earliest days living with my parents and grandparents, wrapped in the quiet love of their home.

Not long after, we moved to Hastings, a place etched in my memory with the charm of childhood: a rope swing stretched across the slopes of a small valley just across the road, the crunch of snowy mornings underfoot and the ever-present, comforting grey skies that seemed to watch over us like an old friend.

When I was five, we moved again, this time to Worthing. For the next six years, Worthing and Hastings were the only two towns I truly knew. They held my childhood stories and rhythms of life.

But then, everything changed.

We moved to South Africa.

The shift was more than just geography; it was a reorientation of everything familiar. New cultures, new sounds, new ways of life. The skies were brighter, the sun stronger, the landscapes wider and wilder. And in some ways, so was I. A part of my foundation was shaped by that early transplanting, uprooting, but also replanting in something that would ultimately grow deep roots of its own.

It was a whole new world – sun-soaked, unfamiliar and utterly foreign to us. From the moment we arrived, it was disorienting. Signs everywhere mentioned an extra charge called GST, which had to be paid on top of the displayed prices. We had no idea what that was. We just knew we had to pay it. Everything felt strange. Even the language was different. Afrikaans filled the air with unfamiliar sounds, making us feel like strangers in a place that didn't quite make room for us yet. But we soon found out it was also the land of braais (barbecues), *'boerewors'* (a long, coiled sausage – the translation is 'farmers sausage') and *'koeksisters'* dripping with golden syrup (a beloved South African sweet treat with a rich cultural heritage. They are deep-fried plaited dough pastries soaked in a cold, sticky syrup, crispy and golden on the outside, soft and syrupy on the inside).

Our first school in South Africa was another shock. We weren't used to the heat. We'd line up in neat rows outside on the hot tarmac, the sun blazing down. Our little English feet just couldn't take it. The ground was scorching. We'd get blisters from just standing still. I remember trying to lift one foot at a time off the ground to stop the burn. My mum would bandage up our feet at home, trying to protect us from a land we hadn't yet grown used to. It was intense and strange, but we were adapting.

Thankfully, we didn't stay in that first place for long. We moved again, this time to a home where we would settle more permanently. That house brought stability. It also brought joy. In our backyard was a swimming pool, cool and sparkling beneath the South African sun. That pool became a place of laughter, joy and relief from the hot sun. We made memories there. Good ones.

That pool also became a place of transformation, where we saw many African believers baptised right there at our home. It was a powerful thing to witness lives surrendering to Jesus so personally. My own baptism took place in a large church in Pretoria after I had given my life to Jesus as a young girl. I was around eleven years old when I took that step of obedience and faith.

There was something beautiful about that season. Even in the strangeness and the stretching, it felt like roots were beginning to form. The land was different, but slowly, we began to find our place in it.

Miracles in Mamelodi

South Africa became the place where some of the most defining memories of my childhood were made. And it was there that I began to see glimpses of courage, calling and even miracles.

My dad had a heart for the people in the African townships. He would often go out to places like Mamelodi, near

Pretoria, to preach, encourage and bring food. He was a living example of his faith. He stepped into communities that were struggling and chose to show up with hope in his hands. I was told of the times he stood in the dust and heat, among people hungry not only for physical bread, but to hear about the love of God, hungry for spiritual nourishment.

One day, we went with him.

It's a day my mum never forgot and one she would've rather not repeated. She hadn't planned for us to be caught in something so intense. That day, tensions were high. The ANC had begun ramping its resistance against apartheid and violence often followed. We were there in the township when the noise started, voices, footsteps, the unmistakable rhythm of a march. My mum heard the sound of people gathering, chanting, building toward what felt like a rising storm.

She stood in that house, gripped with fear, thinking, *Why did I bring the girls here? Why did I bring the children?* My sister Sarah and I were still so young. Anything could've happened. But in that moment, my mum did what she knew best: she prayed.

She tells the story with awe, because as suddenly as the sounds had begun, they shifted. The war cry, the footsteps, the tension, they walked away. It was a miracle. We were safe. Protected.

And perhaps another miracle was this: neither Sarah nor I carry a single memory of that incident. All that we remember is the joy of playing with the African children in the dusty front yard of their bright blue, box-like house. What might have been a traumatic turning point in our young lives simply passed by us. Shielded. Covered. Protected by God.

That day marked something in me. I do not remember that day, but as my mum retold this story, I knew that our family has a God who is faithful to hear our prayers, even in the dust of Mamelodi.

Dust, Discounts and the Long Road Home

After South Africa, we moved again, this time to Australia. I still remember trying to get used to the Aussie slang – cheery *"G'days"* from strangers in the supermarket, words I didn't quite understand but smiled at anyway. We stayed in migrant flats for six weeks, sharing space and stories with others who were also navigating the strange in-between of 'just arrived' and 'not yet settled.'

I didn't like moving. I never really did.

Eventually, we found ourselves settled in Adelaide, where for a year, I got to taste a bit of stability. I made friends in the local youth group and started to feel like I could breathe a little. But just as I was beginning to settle, we moved again. My dad had been offered a job in Coober Pedy.

I've mentioned Coober Pedy earlier, a place famous for its opals, underground homes and searing heat. At other times, it could be described as the land of relentless flies, swirling red dust and supermarket discounts so out of date they were probably a health risk! Dad became the local pastor of the Assembly of God church there and we moved into the church manse, a word not often heard these days, but it simply meant the pastor's house, tucked right next to the church building itself.

By the time I was nineteen, I had lived in three countries, attended five different schools and moved house seven times. Each place left its mark, some with joy, some with tears, all with growth. Looking back, I can see God's hand weaving a story even then, preparing me to understand what it meant to find inheritance in places I never expected.

A Treasure in the Outback

It was in that dry and dusty place, Coober Pedy, with its dust storms, blazing sun and peculiar charm, that I found my greatest earthly treasure. Among the red rocks and underground homes, I met Darren, who became my best friend, my husband and the love of my life.

Darren was an opal miner by trade, but also served as a court orderly. He wore his badge with pride, which cheekily identified him as 'The Sheriff', a title he embraced with a glint in his eye and a sense of duty.

I'll never forget the story from when he first started that job. It was his first day working alone when a magistrate told him that a particular prisoner was to be remanded in custody. But somehow, that detail flew straight over Darren's head and he let the man go. He probably thought that was his lucky day! Hours later, when everyone realised the prisoner had absconded, the police were called to round him up. There, quite oblivious to what was going on around him, he was found celebrating with a drink at the local pub.

Darren laughed about it later, as did everyone else, but that moment sums him up in so many ways: good-hearted, unassuming, willing to step into new roles even when unsure and always ready to grow. Underneath it all was a man of kindness, depth and loyalty.

In a place known for hidden gems beneath rough ground, I found one above it.

Do You Wanna Go for a Feed?

True to his down-to-earth Aussie nature, Darren asked me out in the most classic way possible: 'Do you wanna go for a feed?' It was simple, direct and unmistakably him. I said yes.

That night, we went to the Underground Restaurant, one of Coober Pedy's iconic spots, carved right into the earth, much like the town itself. I thought it was just the two of us. A quiet meal, maybe a chance to get to know each other better.

But as soon as we sat down, in walked Darren's grandparents and then some of their friends. One by one, they poured in like it was a pre-arranged gathering. There I was, suddenly on display for the whole clan!

Well, the cat was well and truly out of the bag.

Whether planned or 'accidental', that night turned into more than just a first date. It was a kind of introduction to the wider family and perhaps, in a way, the beginning of something deeper and more permanent.

Despite the surprise, I couldn't help but smile. It was chaotic, real and a little bit hilarious... just like life in the outback. And somehow, it felt right. Because even in the most unexpected places, love has a way of finding you and planting itself firmly in the soil, ready to grow.

Thirty Years of Covenant Love

In 1995, Darren and I stood at the altar and made a covenant before God and each other. Now this year, we celebrated our 30th wedding anniversary. Three decades of learning, growing, persevering and being held together by grace.

I remember our wedding day so vividly. The photo taken just after the ceremony still takes my breath away: a rainbow stretched over the river in Murray Bridge, arching behind us like a divine signature across the sky. That rainbow was more than just beautiful; it was symbolic. A reminder of God's faithfulness, His covenant of love and His presence in our union from the very beginning.

My father walked me down the aisle that day and he was also the one who officiated our wedding, a moment deeply etched in my heart. I can still hear the emotion in his voice when he asked, 'Who gives this woman to be married to this man?' And then, without missing a beat, he stepped aside and said, 'I do.' A father's love and a pastor's blessing, all wrapped into one unforgettable moment.

Marriage is not always easy. It's a journey of two imperfect people learning how to become one, through storms and sunshine, joy and sorrow, agreement and difference. But if God remains at the centre, if His Spirit guides your choices and His grace covers your gaps, there is a rich inheritance in a marriage that endures.

We've learned over the years that true unity isn't about sameness, it's about oneness in Christ. Decisions aren't made in isolation but as one heart, one mind, under one Lord. And that Scripture still holds us:

> ...what God has joined together,
> let no one separate.
>
> Mark 10:9 NIV

Our marriage is a testimony, not of our perfection, but of God's enduring covenant love. And for that, I am forever grateful.

The Child I Didn't Hold

Our first child was a miscarriage. I don't often say it like that, but it's true. My journey into motherhood didn't begin with a birth; it began with a loss.

I was in Coober Pedy when it happened. A remote, red-dirt town in the middle of South Australia, where life is quiet and rugged. The Royal Flying Doctor Service was called and I was flown out to Port Augusta. It felt like such a big moment happening in such a vast and lonely place.

The hospital I arrived at was a large country hospital. They placed me in a ward with six or eight others, most of them elderly. I remember lying in that room, surrounded by the sounds of coughing, the beeping of machines and the quiet murmur of conversations I didn't belong to. It felt less like a hospital and more like an old people's home. I was the young one, alone in a world that didn't make sense.

I remember lying there, overwhelmed. But grief does strange things; it softens you toward others. I began talking to the woman next to me. She had some kind of disease, she couldn't walk and she had a catheter. And I thought to myself, *I'm grateful. It's not that bad.*

Then a nurse came to check on me and in passing, she told me she'd had seven or eight miscarriages herself. I was stunned. Seven or eight. Again, I thought, *I'm grateful. This is not that bad.*

The night was hard. A patient with a mental health condition was brought in, screaming and unsettled. They moved her out eventually, but the chaos lingered.

Later, a strong, unpleasant smell filled the room. I kept asking the nurse, 'What is that smell?' She asked me to check my bag, but I knew it wasn't me. A day or so later, we discovered the commode chair hadn't been cleaned out. It was such a surreal detail, almost comedic in the way suffering can pile on itself. When it rains, it pours.

But then Darren came down from Coober Pedy. And in the middle of everything, I felt relieved. I wasn't alone anymore.

That chapter didn't end the way I hoped it would. I never got to hold that baby. But I did carry life. And I carried love. And I carried gratitude, because even in loss, I found perspective. Even in pain, I found reasons to be grateful. And even in a ward that smelled like a forgotten chair, I found grace.

To anyone who's experienced loss like this: God sees you. And I want to say, there's still life. There's always life. It may look different from what you imagined, but it will come. Even if it begins with something to be grateful for.

Dancing in the Rain

Some losses leave a quiet ache. Others come suddenly, unexpectedly and leave you holding the weight of what could have been. That's what the ectopic pregnancy felt like. We had already been blessed with two children, Tim and Hannah.

I'd come down to Adelaide for what was meant to be a routine check. Nothing major, just a few symptoms the doctors wanted to follow up on. I went to the Victor Harbor Hospital for a scan and it was there that the tone shifted. The sonographer looked concerned and said words I still remember: 'Go straight to the Women's and Children's Hospital.' As I write this, I hear the words 'Do not pass go.' That humorous Monopoly phrase rings in my ears as I write this. It just seems to go together! There was no time to delay.

I arrived at the Women's and Children's Hospital, but was told to return early the next morning. They admitted me and suddenly, it all became real. It was New Year's Eve, the eve of the year 2000. The world was buzzing with talk about Y2K. People were bracing for computer crashes, banking failures and planes falling out of the sky. But I was bracing for something much more personal. I was about to have surgery to remove an ectopic pregnancy. We all wondered if the hospital would be affected and whether operations would come to a halt. We wondered how much chaos might be caused by the turning of the year into a new millennium.

It was a laparoscopy. Everything went as planned. No computers shut down. The world kept turning. At that time, I remember wondering why our promised child had passed away.

But God met me. He always does.

That Sunday, I went to church, still healing, still sore, still trying to make sense of all that had happened. I carried a quiet ache in my soul, but God met me there. And during worship, we sang *Holy Spirit Rain Down*. [1] As the music filled the church, something in my spirit began to soften and open. In that place of worship, I felt the gentle presence of God beginning to minister to my heart. It was as if heaven leaned in, whispering hope. The words brought to mind a powerful truth from Scripture that was echoed in the lyrics of the song:

> ...No eye has seen, no ear has heard, and no mind has imagined what God has prepared for those who love Him.
>
> 1 Cor 2:9 NLT

In that moment, I held onto the promise that God wasn't finished. That, beyond the pain, there is always more. And the rain, His Spirit was beginning to fall. I began to experience something supernatural. My heart was healed, the sadness lifted and the pain completely vanished in that instant! God was raining down peace. His presence. His promise. It was as if He were saying, I see you. I know what you've lost. And I have something prepared beyond what you can see.

Not long after, I became pregnant again, with our third child, Josh. A new beginning. A promise fulfilled.

Sometimes, God doesn't take us *out* of the storm. He teaches us how to dance in the rain. And through every drop of loss, I've found this to be true: even in pain, He prepares joy.

A Prayer for you today

Lord, I lift up every person who has lost a baby, who feels the ache of empty arms, who is waiting and longing for a child. Meet them right where they are. Wrap them in Your comfort and let them feel Your presence in the middle of their pain.

Bring hope into their grief and may they remember that,

> ...Weeping may last through the night, but joy comes with the morning
>
> Ps 30:5 NLT

I pray for inheritance, whatever form it takes. Whether through children, spiritual family or new beginnings, bless them with what You've prepared.

Give them strength to trust You, grace to find gratitude and joy even in the waiting. Teach them to dance in the rain, believing that life can still spring forth.

Amen.

> 'Sing, barren woman,
> you who never bore a child;
> burst into song, shout for joy,
> you who were never in labour;
> because more are the children of the desolate
> woman than of her who has a husband,'
> says the Lord.
>
> Isa 54:1 NIV

Justice, Joy and the Heart of God

Right now, I find myself in a beautiful and fulfilling season. I have the privilege of supporting my daughter and her growing family, cherishing every moment I spend with my grandchild.

I also have the joy of coming alongside my sister-in-law at times, to help care for our nieces, three of whom are fostered, each a precious life with a story unfolding.

In addition, I've been given the opportunity to volunteer from home for two remarkable organisations: *Ping Pong-A-Thon* and *Wycliffe Bible Translators Australia*. Both, in their own ways, reflect the heartbeat of God, bringing light, hope and transformation to places that desperately need them.

Ping Pong-A-Thon is an inspiring movement that brings communities together through table tennis to raise both awareness and funds in the fight against modern-day slavery. There are estimated to be forty to fifty million men, women, teens and children in the world today who are in slavery.'[2] That reality is almost beyond comprehension.

One of the children who has been rescued through this organisation is little Matthew, only two years old. Matthew had been sold into slavery by his parents and was forced to beg on the streets for 14 hours a day. He was deliberately underfed to evoke pity from passersby. Thankfully, he was rescued from this situation.

The story of little Matthew, sold into slavery and forced to beg on the streets, struck a deep and painful chord in my heart, especially now, as I hold my own grandson in my arms. He is about the same age as Matthew was when that unimaginable injustice occurred. It's almost unbearable to think of the contrast: one child safe, nurtured and deeply loved... and another, deliberately starved and exploited. I cannot fathom how any child could be treated in such a cruel way. It breaks something inside of me.

Every time I look at my grandson's innocent eyes and hear his laughter, I'm reminded of the preciousness of every child and how urgently we must act to protect, defend and fight for the vulnerable. Because no child should ever have to suffer what Matthew did.

The words of Micah 6:8 NKJV come to mind:

> He has shown you, O man, what is good. And what does the Lord require of you?

> But to do justly, to love mercy and to walk
> humbly with your God.

God's heart beats for the nations. From the bustling cities of Asia to remote desert towns, from foster children in Australia to vulnerable children across the globe – He sees, He knows and He cares deeply.

This is the God I serve. The one who invites us into His mission and equips ordinary people to do extraordinary things in His name. This is my inheritance. To stand, speak and serve where God calls. To care for the vulnerable.

Treasures of the Word

While Ping Pong-A-Thon fights for freedom through table tennis, Wycliffe takes up a different weapon, Bible translation, to bring lasting transformation to hearts and nations.

Wycliffe Bible Translators Australia is an organisation with a profound vision: 'to see people from every language group living as disciples of Jesus Christ through the power of God's Word in a language that speaks to their heart.' [3] 'When someone receives the Bible in their own heart language, it's like lifting a full, open cup of water to their lips—refreshing, life-giving and deeply satisfying.'[4]

That vision stirs something deep within me.

We are so incredibly blessed. As I look at my bookshelf, I see the beautiful Bible my grandparents gifted to us when we got married. Next to it sits a variety of other translations, commentaries and bible study guides. And then we have the You Version Bible app, offering instant access to more translations than I can count.

We see in the book of Revelation a powerful picture of what's to come:

> After this I looked, and there before me was
> a great multitude that no one could count,
> from every nation, tribe, people and language,
> standing before the throne and before the
> Lamb...
>
> Rev 7:9 NIV

That verse is the heartbeat of Bible translation. Every tongue. Every tribe. Every dialect. Worshipping together, unified in Christ.

The reason I speak of places and stories of people across the globe is that the nations are part of our inheritance. Psalm 2:8 NIV says,

> Ask me, and I will make the nations your
> inheritance, the ends of the earth your
> possession.

Although this is a Messianic promise from God's heart to His own Son, we, as joint-heirs with Jesus (Rom 8:16-17), can also ask in His Name for the nations, believing that people all over the world will come to know Him. This isn't just for missionaries or global organisations, it's for all of us who follow Christ. God's heart beats for the whole world. I want to gently encourage you: don't limit your vision to your own church, your own community or your own familiar circle. Lift your eyes. There is a world that God loves so deeply. full of people waiting to hear His name, to hold His Word and to know they are seen. When we pray, give, go or serve with the nations in mind, we step into something eternal.

Every nation, every heart and every home carries its own melody of faith. Mine began with an old family piano, full of history, a symbol of worship passed down through generations.

The Modern Day Parable of the Piano

Sometimes, when the house is quiet, I love to sit at the piano and just play. It's one of the ways I worship.

The piano in our home is more than just an instrument; it's a treasured heirloom that once belonged to my grandma. It has journeyed across continents, from England to South Africa and finally to Australia. It carries the sound of our family's legacy within its keys. My mum and three of her siblings all learned to play as children. While growing up in Malawi, there was no TV reception and when the family later moved to the UK, they were given a choice: a television or a piano. They chose the piano. It was familiar, comforting and already woven into the rhythm of their lives. My dad also played it and now, each note that rings out reminds me of the worship that has risen from our family for generations.

Yet over time, life had worn it down. Keys that once sang with joy were now dull and flat. The harmonies, once vibrant, sounded strained. The piano was no longer what it was meant to be.

So we called in the piano tuner. He came quietly, with capable hands and a gentle touch, inspecting every string, every key. Some strings needed tightening. Others had to be replaced. Some notes needed to be tuned and then tuned again. A few broken parts required restoration. It wasn't a quick fix, but it took time, attention and care.

But when he finished, he stepped back, smiled and said,

> The piano is happy again.

I couldn't help but think - that's us.

We were created to live in harmony with God, to be an instrument of His praise and beauty. But life wears us down. The strings of our hearts go out of tune. But we too, have a Master Tuner. His name is Jesus. He comes to restore. To re-tune. He wants to sing His song over us and through us!

Just like my piano, sometimes one tune-up isn't enough. Sometimes double-tuning is required. Sometimes brokenness must be replaced with brand-new strings of truth. But He is patient. He is committed to the restoration process. He fills our lives with joy again and we become a song that brings peace, hope and beauty to those around us.

Zephaniah 3:17 NLT tells us that,

> ...He will take delight in you with gladness.
> With His love, he will calm all your fears.
> He will rejoice over you with joyful songs.

Let Him tune your heart and fill you with joy today. That's your inheritance!

Journal entry 2018

Reflection

Have you considered what inheritance God might be calling you to, perhaps even to the nations?

Are there places, people groups or causes that stir your heart? Ask God to show what steps of faith He might be leading you to take.

In what areas of your life do you sense God is 'tuning' you like an old piano and bringing joy back into your soul? How can you trust His work in your life and become His song of joy and hope for others?

How can you live today in a way that makes an eternal difference?

Chapter 12

Honouring God

Timothy

Names of Inheritance!

In the Bible, names are never just labels; they are declarations of purpose, destiny and inheritance. The names we give and receive carry meaning. As part of our legacy, the Lord has blessed us with children and grandchildren whose names are not random, but purposeful. These three chapters are dedicated to our children, Timothy, Hannah and Joshua.

The Adventurer with the Gospel Up His Sleeve

Tim's name means one who honours God. It is a mantle he quietly wears. Just as Paul called Timothy his 'true son in the faith' (1 Tim 1:2), our Tim walks with strength, integrity and loyalty. He carries a teachable heart and the steadiness of a spiritual son called to build and lead.

Tim has always carried an adventurous spirit. Whether it's metal detecting in the bush or exploring the depths through what I can only describe as a kind of underwater escapade, not quite deep-sea diving, but something daring nonetheless, he's always been curious, always exploring. When he was a boy, we saw that curiosity bloom in the most unexpected ways.

Curiosity and Rings of Steel

I remember one day he was sitting quietly in the shed, watching his dad work away at his upholstery. He must have been about eight. He would sit for hours just observing, soaking in every movement, every tool. One day, a pair of shiny eyelets caught his eye. To him, they looked like beautiful, blingy rings, so naturally, he slipped two of them onto his fingers. They were thick and ridged and before long, we realised... they weren't coming off.

Darren came rushing in, telling me the rings were stuck. His solution? Cut them off...with a grinder. I said 'Absolutely not!' and off we raced to the hospital. Coober Pedy is a remote community with limited resources and at that time, we had only a locum doctor. He looked at the eyelets, not knowing what to do. The ring cutter wouldn't cut through because they were too thick. That's when the nurse got serious. She told us to hold Tim's arms up so the blood would drain down and reduce the swelling. Then she returned with urgency, speaking with authority to this locum doctor who did not seem to have the experience to deal with this extraordinary situation: 'We need to get these off pronto or we're flying him out – he could lose his fingers.'

Finally, the hospital maintenance man came in with a Dremel, a high-speed, handheld rotary power tool. Slowly, carefully and with plenty of pauses to cool the metal in water, they cut those rings free. I'll never forget the relief or the lessons learned about imagination and curiosity that day.

Arrows that Missed the Mark

And then there was the infamous *shish kebab* incident. One afternoon, Tim came inside with a strange look on his face and two long kebab sticks sticking out of his hands. I thought he was joking. He wasn't. He had been experimenting with a homemade slingshot and the projectiles didn't launch as expected. Instead, they went straight into the back of his hands. Back to the hospital we went, but thankfully, there was no lasting damage. The nurse had a good laugh that day and dubbed him 'the emergency room shish kebab'. Boys will be boys, especially when they're born to test boundaries and imagine new possibilities.

As a Boy!

Even before all that, Tim had a heart for Jesus. When he was little, he had a treasured Bible storybook we used to read together. He called it his 'Jesus Book'. He would flip through the pages, pointing at every character and confidently declaring,'There's Jesus! There's Jesus!' It didn't matter if it was Moses, David or an angel – he saw Jesus in every story. And maybe, in a way, that simple faith captured something profound: the heart of a child who instinctively recognised God's presence in every moment, every page, every part of the story.

Tim has grown from a boy of curiosity into a man of strength and conviction. But Tim's real treasure hunting happens as he digs deep into the things of God. These days, the books on his shelf are the kind that make me tilt my head and smile, rich with apologetics, deep theology and philosophical reflections that sometimes go right over my head. But Tim doesn't keep that knowledge to himself. He shares Jesus in the most simple, disarming, natural way, chatting with his neighbour who's Hindu or Muslim, with gentleness, clarity and conviction. He's on fire for God, but you'd never hear him shout about it. You'd just see it in how he lives.

That flame started early. From the time he was only four, Tim would lovingly ask people, 'Do you know Jesus?' Whether it was the person sitting at the next table in a restaurant or someone in the waiting room at the doctor's surgery, it didn't matter who it was. He wasn't shy about the treasure he'd found. He just wanted others to find it too.

His real treasure is found in the field of great price!

A Magician with a Mission

These days, Tim is a magician, not just with sleight of hand (though he has quite the collection of clever tricks), but with the way he brings joy, wonder and the unexpected into everyday moments. It's almost poetic that the same fingers that once got stuck in shiny metal rings now move with precision and delight to entertain and inspire, causing rings to disappear at the astonishment of those watching.

And now, I suspect, a far more meaningful ring may be on his mind. Perhaps soon, one of those hands will be holding a ring not for play or performance, but for promise. A proposal may just be around the corner. From stuck eyelets to sleight of hand, to slipping a ring onto someone's left hand in love, God's hand has always been at work in Tim's story.

I had already written this part of Tim's story, but before I published it, this beautiful daughter of promise was engaged to our Tim. Her name is Zoe, meaning 'life' and her favourite verse is the same as mine. I can only think that God will place His desires in their hearts, as they too delight themselves in the Lord, become one and journey together into the inheritance that God has for them. We are looking forward to this new season with a new daughter joining our family. It's such an exciting time for us all. What a treasure Tim has found in Zoe!

A Sword from the Water

Perhaps one of the most defining moments of Tim's life came underground, both literally and spiritually. He was baptised in Coober Pedy at Faye's Underground Home, a tourist spot carved into the rock, complete with a swimming pool built deep beneath the surface. It was winter and the water wasn't exactly warm that day, but what happened was nothing short of powerful. All of Tim's grandparents were there to witness a moment of deep obedience as he chose to publicly follow Jesus.

As Tim came up from the water, my dad, his grandpa, saw a vision. He saw Tim rise from the water, a sword in his hand. That image struck us all. It wasn't just poetic; it was prophetic. A symbol of God's power and calling on Tim's life – sharp, purposeful and forged in surrender. That day, underground in the cold, a warrior emerged and we knew: Tim would be used by God in a mighty way.

The Inheritance Continues

Tim lives as if every moment is a divine appointment. He's been placed here, now, for such a time as this. He is part of our legacy. He is our son. *Springs and Stones* is about women who stood their ground for inheritance and I see in Tim a spring that flows from my life into his. A promise passed on, not in theory, but in life. From me to him and one day, through him, to his own children.

> Like arrows in the hand of a warrior are the children of one's youth.
>
> Ps 127:4 ESV

He has always aimed high, even when the arrows didn't always fly straight. But God, the true archer, is shaping his aim. Tim is an arrow with purpose, a spring from a source much deeper than he knows, part of a story that is still unfolding.

> Timothy, my dear son, be strong through the grace God gives you in Christ Jesus.
>
> 2 Tim 2:1 NLT

Reflection

Are you looking for opportunities to love the person in front of you, even in the ordinary places? At the shops, at home, in waiting rooms. How can you carry God's presence into those places?

What 'treasure' has God placed within you that you can offer to others? Is it an encouraging word, a prayer, a listening ear, a home-cooked meal or a simple offer of 'how can I help you today?'

Chapter 13

Grace

Hannah

'Grace' or 'Favour'

Hannah's name speaks of divine favour and answered prayer. Like the Hannah of Scripture, her life carries grace for others and strength in surrender. She is a woman of worship and sacrifice and a carrier of promise.

As she grew, I saw in her so many characteristics that reflected the very image of God: loving, caring, sweet, diligent, kind, faithful, thoughtful, creative and hardworking. She is a joy to be around, a light in every room she enters.

Her name means grace, a word so simple, yet so profound. Grace is the unearned, undeserved, unmerited favour of God, freely given to us through what Jesus accomplished at the cross. It is not something we can earn by our goodness; it is God's gift of love to us.

Ephesians 2:8-9 ESV reminds us:

> For by grace you have been saved through faith. And this is not your own doing; it is the gift of God, not a result of works, so that no one may boast.

Hannah's life is a testimony to that grace. She doesn't strive to impress or perform to earn love—she simply carries it. Like a spring of living water, her kindness and faithfulness flow naturally, not from effort, but from identity. She is a woman marked by grace and through her, many have tasted and seen the goodness of God.

Pillars in the House of the Lord

Hannah is married to Jakin, a name that carries deep prophetic meaning: 'He will establish.' Found in the temple language of 1 Kings and echoed in Revelation 3:12, Jakin symbolises a strong pillar in the house of the Lord. 1 Kings 7:21 NIV describes these pillars in King Solomon's temple:

> He erected the pillars at the portico of the temple. The pillar to the south he named Jakin and the one to the north Boaz.

Jakin, like the pillars of the temple, is strong, faithful and steadfast, leading, providing for, and loving his family well, with a heart devoted to Jesus and worship.

Together, Hannah and Jakin are being established in strength, rooted in grace and building God's kingdom!

When I created a prayer poster combining the meanings of their names, with heartfelt input from Jakin's mother, Angela, we saw a legacy unfolding, a family established in spiritual strength, unwavering faith and generational blessing. Their union speaks of a foundation not only for their own lives but for those who come after them.

> The one who is victorious I will make a pillar in the temple of my God. Never again will they leave it. I will write on them the name of my God and the name of the city of my God, the new Jerusalem, which is coming down out of heaven from my God; and I will also write on them my new name.
>
> Rev 3:12 NIV

It is no surprise, then, that their home is filled with grace, with worship and with the presence of God. Hannah and Jakin are not just continuing a legacy; they are building upon it. They are writing a new chapter of faith for their own children, marked by surrender and grace.

At their wedding, that legacy was beautifully honoured. Just as my father officiated our wedding, it was Jakin's grandfather, Peter, who stood to bless and join Hannah and Jakin in marriage. A pastor himself, Peter spoke with authority, carrying the richness of inheritance and blessing to the next generation. It was more than a celebration; it was a moment of prophetic significance, when heaven's blessing rested tangibly on a couple who carry the weight and wonder of legacy with grace.

Through this beautiful promise is the assurance of inheritance, not just for today, but for their children and their children's children. This is a blessing for you, too!

> The Lord bless you and keep you;
> The Lord make His face shine upon you
> and be gracious to you;
> The Lord turn His face toward you
> and give you peace.
>
> Num 6:24–26 NIV

Along comes Ezekiel Peter!

It was the seventh day of the seventh month when Ezekiel was born. Remarkably, both of his parents share this pattern: Hannah was born on the 7th of February and Jakin on the 7th of January. Three lives, each beginning on the seventh day. In biblical numerology, the number seven is significant and symbolises completion, fullness and spiritual perfection.

It was on the seventh day that God rested from all His work of creation (Gen 2:2). Not because He was tired, but because it was finished. Complete. Whole. And in that same spirit, Ezekiel's birth feels like God was declaring, 'This is good. This is right. This is My perfect timing.'

We are reminded in Psalm 139:13-14 NIV of the intricate care with which God forms each life:

> For you created my inmost being; you knit me together in my mother's womb. I praise you because I am fearfully and wonderfully made; your works are wonderful, I know that full well.

Ezekiel's name is a prophetic declaration: 'God will strengthen.' He represents the continuation of the spiritual legacy and the promise that God will empower the next generation.

Ezekiel is a bundle of joy, full of energy and laughter. His very presence lights up a room. As I look at him, I can't help but wonder what destiny is being written by the hand of God in his life. What dreams are being planted? What words will he speak? What lives will he touch?

Ezekiel's arrival wasn't just the birth of a baby; it was the unfolding of a promise. A seventh-day rest. A holy punctuation mark in the story of generational grace. He is living proof that God's timing is perfect, His designs are intentional and His legacy never fails.

Micah: God's Gift of Mercy

It was near the completion of this book that our second grandson, little Micah Jakin, was born. His name means, 'Who is like our God?' In Scripture, Micah was a prophet who spoke boldly about justice and urged the people to 'act justly, love mercy and walk humbly with God' (Mic 6:8). True to his name, Micah also turned the question back in worship, declaring,

> Who is a God like you,
> who pardons sin and forgives the
> transgression of the remnant of his inheritance?
> You do not stay angry forever
> but delight to show mercy.
> You will again have compassion on us;
> you will tread our sins underfoot
> and hurl all our iniquities into the
> depths of the sea…
>
> Micah 7:18-20 NIV

As this new life grows, may he reflect the meaning of his name, showing to the world around him the goodness and mercy of our God. We don't yet know the plans God has for Micah's life, but we do know that he was 'knit together' by the Lord even before he was born (Ps 139:13). We look forward with joy to seeing him smile, crawl, walk and talk. Even now, we already know he is a precious gift from God and through his little life, we see how God is blessing our family.

Micah, we love you already!

Overflowing Grace

As a mother, I always tried to keep things neat and tidy. I suppose part of that came from a desire for peace in the home, a sense of order amidst the chaos of raising children. But I'll admit, when something spilled, whether it was milk, water or juice, it often spilled something in me too. A bit of stress, a quick word, an urge to clean it all up before it soaked in too deep. I wanted calm, not mess. But what I didn't realise back then was that those spills were showing me something: that whatever comes out when we're bumped is what's already inside us.

There's a beautiful analogy I once heard: when a cup is bumped, whatever's inside spills out. It's not the bump that causes the mess; it's what's already in the cup. And I've been thinking about that in light of the springs the Bible speaks of, the living water flowing from within us. What spills out when life knocks us a little? What overflow are we carrying?

Jesus said in John 7:38, 'Whoever believes in me, as Scripture has said, rivers of living water will flow from within them.' (NIV) This verse speaks of the overflow that belief produces. Living water. Grace. Patience. Joy. The kind of abundance that doesn't shut down at a mess, but instead makes space for wonder.

My daughter has taught me so much about this. Watching her with her little one has been like seeing a new way of being a mother. Where I once saw mess, she sees opportunity. Where I would have rushed to mop up the milk or shut down the puddle-making, she leans in. She lets her son pour, spill, squish and explore, not because she doesn't care about cleanliness, but because she sees the value in the mess. She sees learning. She sees life.

To her, these are moments of wonder. A spilled cup isn't an accident; it's an invitation. A chance for him to know the world and know himself. And instead of rushing to stop the overflow, she welcomes it. Because even in the mess, His grace is there and overflowing love pours out.

Inheritance that Flows

Our children are living testimonies of God's faithfulness. They are stones of remembrance and springs of hope, flowing from one generation to another. Through them, the legacy continues. Through them, the story is still being written.

Reflection

When life 'bumps' you, what is flowing out of your cup? Is it peace or pressure, grace or frustration? What do those moments reveal about what's filling your heart?

Are you discovering God's grace even in the messy, unplanned or unfinished moments of your life? What might He be teaching you?

Where have you seen God's favour quietly at work in your life, perhaps in unexpected ways, relationships or timing?

Chapter 14

Our Youngest Olive Shoot

Josh

Josh, the youngest of our olive shoots, is full of spirit and grit. He's our adventurer, resilient, daring and full of life. From spear fishing and surfing to kayaking, gym workouts and motorbike riding, Josh is never one to sit still. I remember the time he skidded on ice whilst riding his motorbike and weeks of painful healing followed, with sores trailing down his leg. And then there was football, where he dislocated his shoulder, eventually requiring a full shoulder reconstruction. He's certainly the strongest, in body and will.

He is so different from Tim and Hannah, each of them a unique branch from the same tree. As a young child, Josh was wonderfully cuddly. If you have a child like that, treasure those moments, because as they grow older, those warm snuggles may become less frequent. These days, I feel especially blessed when I get a hug from him as he towers over me now and in those moments, I still see my little boy.

One particular evening stands out in my memory. Josh had gone kayaking and, as always, had told me where he was heading. But as night fell, I couldn't get hold of him and my worry began to rise. I called Darren, my husband, who was working away at the mine. He calmly but seriously told me, 'If he doesn't answer soon, you'll need to call the police. It's getting dark and finding him won't be easy.' Just after that call, Josh finally rang. I let him know just how worried we'd been and how close we'd come to making that call. It was a moment that reminded me just how precious he is.

Josh has always been our most adventurous child, though Tim certainly gives him a run for his money. I'll never forget the time Josh, just four years old, vanished into the hills of Coober Pedy. I was at work and Darren was busy doing upholstery in his shed, whilst Josh was napping or so he thought! Upon awakening, Josh decided he wanted to go on an adventure and was gone, chasing after our dog, Jock.

Jock was named after *Jock of the Bushveld,* a loyal Staffordshire Bull Terrier who journeyed through the rugged South African wilderness with his master in the late 1800s. That Jock braved wild terrain, wild animals and danger at every turn. It somehow felt fitting that our Jock would be found wandering the hills with our son in tow; two explorers, side by side.

Darren didn't want to alarm me right away, but around our little hilltop community, aptly named Hopeful Hills, the word went out. Friends, family and Darren's parents joined the search. If you know Coober Pedy, you'll understand how frightening that was. The land is riddled with deep, unmarked shafts left behind by opal miners. Signs warning of danger are everywhere. The name itself, *Coober Pedy*, comes from an Aboriginal term meaning 'white man's hole in the ground' and that's exactly what it is. A dangerous place for any child to go missing.

As the sun dipped lower, Brian, my father-in-law heard distant cries. At first, he thought it was the children from the Aboriginal family next door. But then he realised, it was Josh. His faint voice carried from up in the hills, where he was found safe and sound, beside Jock. What a moment of overwhelming relief! Our beautiful treasure, preserved by God's grace.

That day, we truly lived out the promise of Jeremiah 33:3 NIV:

> Call to me and I will answer you and tell you great and unsearchable things you do not know.

We called out to God and He answered. Our little treasure was returned to us, unharmed. When I came home later that day, everything seemed perfectly normal, but I soon knew that a miracle had unfolded. And I give thanks.

A Bold Baptism

When Josh was just eleven, his older sister Hannah decided to be baptised. Inspired by her faith and following God wholeheartedly in his own way, Josh decided he would be baptised too. It was a sincere step for such a young boy and he meant every word.

The pastor at the time wanted to make sure Josh truly understood the decision he was making. Gently, he asked, 'Now, young Josh, what will you do if I don't baptise you?' Without missing a beat, Josh boldly replied, 'Well, I'll baptise myself then.'

That quick and earnest answer was all he needed to hear. It was clear to him that Josh's heart was in it. He was ready.

It was a windy day and the sea was a little rough and nature seemed to join in the excitement. My dad was invited to help baptise them both, alongside their father, Darren. What a special moment to have three generations standing together in the waves, witnessing and partaking in such a beautiful moment.

The waves did more than just crash on the shore that day; they practically helped with the baptisms! The sea, wild and alive, seemed to echo the joy and the washing away of the old life. It didn't take much effort to immerse them; the water was already doing its part.

As I stood there watching my children in the waves, Hannah and Josh making their public declaration of faith, I was reminded again of the power of prayer and generational faith.

That day was more than just a milestone; it was the fruit of many whispered prayers, quiet moments and heartfelt conversations. It was the visible beginning of something deeply rooted.

Now, as my children are talking to Jesus for themselves, I continue talking to Him about them. This is the legacy of faith, not just instructing them in prayer, but living it and letting them see that God is always near and always listening.

It remains one of the most treasured memories in our family, a symbol of new life, of obedience and of a young boy's unshakeable determination to follow Christ, no matter what.

The Feather in his Sock!

A feather. It stopped me in my tracks. It may seem simple to others, but to me, it was a whisper from heaven. I knew what it meant. At that moment, I knew it wasn't ordinary. The Lord whispered to my heart, 'I'm watching over him. I'm guiding him. I'm going with him wherever he treads.' It was as if the Lord was saying, 'even in the small, unseen places. I've already gone before him.'

> Every place that the sole of your foot will tread upon I have given it to you...
>
> Josh 1:3 ESV

That feather, tucked into his sock, represented the very place where his foot would step. It was a divine reminder that God's presence goes with him. God's protection covers him. And God's promise surrounds his every step.

That day, I was overwhelmed by the tenderness of God's love for my son. Even in clean laundry. Even in a sock. Even in a feather.

That feather in his sock became a prophetic picture of God's faithfulness. It was as though the Spirit of God tucked it there Himself, to remind me that He watches over our son, even in the unseen places. The ground he walks on is not uncharted. It's already been promised. Already been prayed for.

There is a beautiful verse in Psalm 85:13 NKJV that promises:

> Righteousness will go before Him, and shall make His footsteps *our* pathway.

This verse talks about God making a way for us to walk in. A way of inheritance, a way of protection, a way that is destined by God for them to walk in. And I believe this for my children and for your children, too. They carry the weight of prayers spoken long before they were born. We've talked to Jesus for our Joshua. And every time I see that feather, I know God has heard.

Joshua – The Lord Saves!

A warrior's name. Joshua carries the inheritance of leadership, boldness and faith. He is a reminder that God raises up deliverers for each generation, those who will walk boldly into promised places and lead others with courage and faithfulness.

> ...But as for me and my house,
> we will serve the Lord.
>
> Josh 24:15 NKJV

Joshua is our son, but even more than that, he belongs to God.

His name carries a destiny: 'The Lord saves.' It echoes the call of the biblical Joshua, who led God's people into their inheritance. And like that Joshua, we've always believed that our son has been marked to walk into promises bigger than himself.

I have prayed many prayers over him. Some spoken aloud. Bold declarations of faith. Some whispered through tears. Some in silence when I had no words. Others in the middle of the night as I knelt by my bed. Every one of them has been part of his inheritance.

Prophetic Declaration: The Joshua Generation

Matt Mongomery describes in his song, *Joshua Generation*, a time for our generation to wake up and step into the destiny God has prepared. [1] For too long, they have been held back by fear, apathy and the illusion of self-sufficiency. But now the call is clear: rise with vision, courage and obedience.

Like Joshua standing at the edge of the Promised Land, this is the hour for our generation to take hold of their inheritance, to lead with boldness and to ignite a fire that will awaken the

Church and transform the world. Like Joshua of old, they are called to lead others into the promises of God, not through fear or compromise, but through wholehearted trust in the One who goes before them.

Our children are living testimonies of God's faithfulness and prophetic destiny. They are stones of remembrance and springs of hope, flowing from one generation to another.

Through them, the legacy continues. Through them, the story is still being written.

'The children you gave us, Lord, are our inheritance. We entrust them back to You. May they walk in the name they carry. Amen'

Reflection

Where Has God Left You a Feather? Sometimes God speaks through His Word. Sometimes through a whisper in prayer. And sometimes... He tucks a feather into a sock.

Has God ever given you a sign like that, a gentle reminder of His presence, His promises or His protection over someone you love? Perhaps it was in a word from a friend, a verse, a song, a dream... At the right moment?

Sometimes it could be in a beautiful photograph of a butterfly with the sun shimmering on its wings. All it takes is to open our eyes and hearts to hear Him. There was no denying, it was a whisper from heaven.

Write it down. What did it mean to you at the time? What did it reveal about God's heart for you or your family?

Remember: Even the smallest signs can point to the deepest truths.

This is also your story! Your prayers are powerful. And your God is faithful.

Chapter 15

A Mother's Prayer

A Prayer for my Child

There is no one who loves and cares for your child more than Jesus! As you pray, I encourage you to place your child's name into this prayer and trust that God hears your heart today. For simplicity, this prayer refers to 'she' and 'her'.

'I lift my child _____ to you, Lord. You know her better than I ever could. You knew her intimately even before she was born. You go before her and guide every step of her life. She is made in your image and you have called her your child.

Father, soften her heart and break down any walls and draw her into Your love today. I pray for the calling and destiny on her life to be fulfilled. Nothing and no one can steal the inheritance that belongs to her in Christ.

I will fight on my knees in prayer, standing firm in faith. At the same time, I rest in Your finished work, knowing that You are holding my child in the palm of Your hand. Even when I cannot see it, I trust that you are working behind the scenes, shaping my child's life into a masterpiece for your glory. I will rest in the assurance that my child is covered by angels who are on assignment, guarding and protecting her life.

Thank you, Holy Spirit, for drawing my child and leading her to the way of salvation. Place within her a deep desire to know Jesus intimately. May she encounter you at the well of salvation. I pray that You will be the only One who satisfies – The Living Water who quenches her soul. May the goodness of God overwhelm her.

Thank you for being her portion. Thank you for the inheritance you have prepared for my child. Thank you for every promise You have spoken over her life.

Amen'

> So will My word be which goes out of My mouth; It will not return to Me void (useless, without result), Without accomplishing what I desire, And without succeeding in the matter for which I sent it.
>
> Isa 55:11 AMP

A MOTHER'S PRAYER

Chapter 16

The Prodigal's Inheritance

As I worked on editing this book, I realised there was a chapter missing – one that needed to be written. There are many who are raised in the ways of God but have wandered away, whether due to life's disappointments, deception, sin, shame or chasing after a life apart from God's best. At times, it can even be a heart of pride and entitlement that pulls them off course!

This chapter is for those who are praying for loved ones to come home. They may have been away for a short while or for many years, but God, in His mercy, is calling them home. May this encourage you in faith, prayer and God's promises, knowing that He loves and cares for your prodigal more than you could ever imagine.

If you haven't grown up in the Christian faith, you may not be familiar with the word *prodigal*. I encourage you to read the story of the Prodigal Son found in Luke 15, which is also known as the Parable of the Loving Father. In this story, a son leaves the security of his loving home, where everything was provided for him and wastes his inheritance on reckless living. Yet when he finally returns, he discovers his father has been waiting with open arms, ready to forgive, embrace and restore him.

The Prodigal King

But there is also another story in the Old Testament about a Prodigal King called Manasseh! This story is found in 2 Chronicles 33:1-20.

As I reflected on his story, I became curious about the kind of family life he experienced while growing up. Much like the prodigal, he lacked nothing. His mother is not mentioned, but his father was Hezekiah, King of Judah. Manasseh grew up in the palace of a father remembered for his righteousness. Hezekiah trusted the Lord and led Judah through reform, tearing down idols, removing high places and calling the nation back to worship God alone.

Manasseh became king when he was a child, only twelve years old and some say that he was 'co-regent with his father for perhaps ten years from the ages of twelve to twenty-two and that he lived in close relationship with him.' [1]

However, Manasseh walked away from God. How disappointing that must have been for his father to watch. He walked in rebellion. He rebuilt all the high places his father had torn down, raised up altars for the Baals and made wooden images. He practised witchcraft, sorcery and consulted mediums and psychics. He even profaned God's temple with idols and sacrificed his own son in the fire.

We read that

> ...He did much evil in the sight of God...
> So Manasseh seduced Judah and all the inhabitants of Jerusalem to do more evil than the nations whom the Lord had destroyed before the children of Israel.
>
> 2 Chr 33:6,9 NKJV

It's hard to understand how he chose such a different path from his father. But God still had a call on his life and in his sovereignty, we read:

> So the Lord brought against them the army commanders of the king of Assyria, who took Manasseh prisoner, put a hook in his nose, bound him with bronze shackles and took him to Babylon.
>
> 2 Chr 33:11 NIV

Manasseh found himself in a prison where he was brought to his knees in repentance and humility! God, in His great mercy, listened to his prayer and brought him back to Jerusalem and it says:

> ...Then Manasseh knew that the Lord is God.
>
> 2 Chr 33:13 NIV

As a result, Manasseh pulled down the idols and we read in the Message that,

> ...He also did a good spring cleaning on The Temple, carting out the pagan idols and the goddess statue. He took all the altars he had set up on the Temple hill and throughout Jerusalem and dumped them outside the city. He put the Altar of God back in working order and restored worship...He issued orders...'You shall serve and worship God, the God of Israel...'
>
> 2 Chr 33:14-17

His repentance encompassed a complete change of heart, a turning away from everything that was not of God. As 2 Corinthians 7:10 NIV reminds us,

> Godly sorrow brings repentance that leads to salvation and leaves no regret, but worldly sorrow brings death.

In Manasseh's story, we witness the mercy and sovereignty of God at work, drawing him back to Himself.

Godly Wisdom in the Waiting!

Waiting for a prodigal to return can feel like one of the most hopeless seasons of life. The days stretch long and the nights are filled with questions, prayers and tears. Yet even in this waiting, there is hope. God has not abandoned your story or the one you love. In fact, His Word is filled with wisdom, strength and promises for such a time as this. I pray that the following wisdom will be helpful for you as you wait.

Standing on God's Word

I have been deeply encouraged by Karen Wheaton's faith and by her daughter Lindsey's powerful testimony of hope. Karen wrote about her youngest daughter coming home in her book, *Watching the Road* and she shares on her website about her decision to stand on the Word of God. She said,

> I would have to accept what the enemy had intended for my daughter, which was to ultimately kill, steal and destroy her life,
>
> OR
>
> I would determine what GOD had to say about her and stand on THAT Word until this situation looked like God's Word. [2]

Her book stands as an encouragement to anyone praying for a prodigal, offering hope in God's promises. She contended in prayer for her daughter during her season of wandering and she witnessed a miracle unfold when her daughter returned home!

Letting Go!

Her daughter, Lindsey Doss, shares her own journey in *The Way Home,* inspiring faith as she recounts how she walked away from God, pursued her own path, but ultimately the miraculous love of God found her and brought her home.[3] She also writes in her blog, *Welcome to the Pig Pen,* about two difficult years where she lived at her lowest point. Lindsey explains,

> The pig pen is where people are brought to their lowest place.. It is who they are without God.[4]

Even though our natural instinct is to intervene when our prodigals walk away from God, there is a purpose in letting them go. Eventually, they will encounter the emptiness of their choices. In the end, they will see the consequences of their actions that have led them to rock bottom. It is at this time that they will realise their deep need for God to bring peace, fulfilment and wholeness.

Although this is not always the case and it can be very hard to watch, we can pray that they come to their senses before reaching such a place. Yet even if they do, God can redeem their story and turn it into a powerful testimony to share with others in the future!

Just a few weeks ago, I heard from a couple of prodigals who shared how far they had fallen. One had struggled with alcoholism to the point of sometimes being found lying in the middle of the road at night. The day he came to church, God delivered him and now he is walking in faith, transformed and renewed. Though he was raised in a Christian home, he had wandered far and still had to make the daily choice to renew His mind in the Word. Another prodigal shared how he had battled suicidal thoughts until he discovered his purpose in God. These stories are living proof that there is hope! No one is beyond the reach of God's love and restoring power.

There are seasons when a child wanders far from home, chasing after worldly things that promise freedom but bring pain and emptiness. Even in the darkness of those wandering nights, God is at work, preparing the way for eventual repentance and the hope of full restoration.

Pray and Contend for their Souls

During this time, prayer is powerful and touches the heart of God. He alone can heal, restore and bring them home. Only He can reach their hearts. There is a time to intercede with authority and passion! In the middle of long nights filled with worry and heartache for a child or any loved one, who wanders far from the safety and guidance of home, the song *Battle Belongs* becomes a powerful war cry. It reminds us that NOTHING IS IMPOSSIBLE FOR GOD, even when circumstances seem hopeless.

He sees beauty in the ashes of their brokenness and when everything looks hopeless, we can fight on our knees, not in our own strength, but fully trusting that the battle belongs to the Lord. [5] In these painful moments, it is easy to feel helpless or sad, but there is something we *can* do: press into God more deeply, pray with persistence and intercede faithfully.

God Himself is Interceding!

We can rest in the truth that God Himself is interceding for our children, understanding them far more deeply than we ever could. He loves them more than we can ever comprehend. He knows them better than we do. His wisdom and love are greater than we can imagine. He is standing in the gap for them and always working behind the scenes!

Trust and Faith

God is working in the unseen and He has a plan to bring them home, just like the Prodigal who came home to the father when he got to the end of himself, and King Manasseh when God brought him to his knees. God is sovereign.

Remaining steadfast in His promises is the key, knowing that He is faithful to act in His perfect timing. Though the process is painful and uncertain, it calls for complete trust.

Though the path is difficult, God's presence is always there. Even in the darkness, He is quietly at work. In those moments, parents may catch glimpses of sorrow on their child's face, a fleeting awareness of the cost of their choices. These glimpses are heart-wrenching, yet they also reveal God's quiet work, stirring their hearts toward reflection, repentance and eventually, return. Often in those times, we can question *why*, especially when we feel we have done everything we can to guide, teach and nurture those we love.

We may at times reflect on moments of regret or things that could have been done differently, but God calls us to look forward. Nothing is wasted! God is weaving every choice into a larger tapestry for His good.

It is His love for each child that allows for free will. Each person must personally respond to the call of God on their life. Thank God that He is bringing His purposes about in a way we cannot understand. He is God and we can trust Him.

Thankfulness and Praise

Simply be thankful! Thankful for them and for what God is doing even when you can't see it. Sandy, my aunty reminds us to 'fix our eyes on Almighty God and see Him in His rightful place of honour and power. When we do this, even in the middle of difficult circumstances, our perspective shifts. Instead of being weighed down by despair, we are lifted into hope as we reflect on the greatness of our God.'

Refiners Fire

This season shapes patience, humility, perseverance and unwavering dependence on the Lord. It teaches us that love is not always about control or fixing, but about faithful prayer, persistent hope and resting in God's timing. Use these times to ask God what He wants to do in you! You will begin to see your heart being moulded to reflect the Father's heart towards

His children. In this, you catch a small glimpse into the depth of God's love for us.

Mercy and Grace

King Manasseh is a powerful example that no one is beyond God's reach. His story reveals God's immense mercy and reminds us that, just as God rescued Manasseh, He extends that same mercy to each one of us. Mercy is described as getting what we don't deserve through what Jesus did at the cross for us, providing a way into His best for us. God could have left Manasseh in that dungeon, with a hook in his nose and shackles on his feet. He didn't. The prodigal son made his way home He didn't remain in the pig pen! God shows us so much mercy. This is why we trust Him.

Sandy shared these thoughts on the lost son in Luke 15,

> When the prodigal got to rock bottom and he came to his senses, he asked himself, 'Why am I here in the pigsty when it could be so different?'. He rehearsed what he would say, 'Father, I was wrong, I have sinned and I'm not worthy to be called your son. I will work as a servant for you.' (Luke 15:17-19) His self-image was damaged. He saw himself as a failure, unworthy of any life other than to be a slave.
>
> But when the Father saw him from a distance, He ran to him. He did not disown him or wait to hear the rehearsed speech. Instead, He embraced

him with deep compassion, hugging this beggar who smelled of pigs and squalor, dressing him in a robe of righteousness and placing a ring on his finger. What amazing grace.

Let us pray that our prodigals may truly understand God's grace and mercy and personally experience the forgiveness and restoration of God.

Expecting their Return!

Before the prodigal even returned, the father was already preparing a feast and 'fattening the calf' (Lk 15:23). He was expectant in the hope that his son was coming home. I am sure fattening a calf was a slow process, not something you could do overnight.

This detail shows us something important. The father had been preparing long before his son's footsteps were heard on that pathway home. He lived in expectation, ready to rejoice the moment it happened.

That's what faith looks like in the waiting. We, too, can anticipate the return of our loved ones with full expectation that God is there waiting to embrace them with open arms. That's the heart of our Father – expectant, ready and waiting!

The story of the Prodigal is a prophetic picture of being fully restored into grace, identity and authority – he comes back as a son, not a slave!

Testimony of Friends and Family

I felt it was important to include testimonies from those who are still in the waiting. They are women who love God deeply and have walked faithfully with Him, yet have watched their children wander far from Him. They continue to stand firm, clinging to God's promises through prayer and praise. These stories remind us that we are not alone, God is always at work, even when we cannot see it yet.

Yvonne's Encouragement!

Yvonne, a dear friend and grandma, shares from her heart to ours..

'The ultimate thing I have learned is to truly TRUST GOD. To know that He KNOWS and LOVES my grown kids more than I ever could. To TRUST the Scripture when it says in Proverbs 22:6 ESV,

> Train up a child in the way he should go; even when he is old he will not depart from it.

I have learned to trust and rely on God – that He will do His part, for He CANNOT lie. A promise I hold onto is from Isaiah 44:3 NIV:

> ...I will pour out my Spirit on your offspring, and my blessing on your descendants.

Pray, praise and truly trust! While I do those three things, I believe God is working to bring about the miracle of salvation of my grown kids and grandkids.'

Sandy's Encouragement

'While waiting let's:

Pray that God reveals to them how precious they are and that they begin to see themselves the way He sees them.

Pray that they receive revelation through dreams and that angels would minister to them.

Pray for the Lord to bring godly, supportive friends into their lives.

Pray against the lies of the enemy and for his lies to fall on deaf ears.

Pray in the Spirit, especially in those moments when you don't know how to pray.

Even before you see the evidence of change, begin to picture them free, rising up as over-comers, mighty men and women of God.'

Reflection

I've been thinking about the different ways God brings His prodigals home. For the son in Jesus' parable, it was hitting rock bottom in the pig pen that turned his heart back to his father. For King Manasseh, it was the chains of captivity that humbled him until he cried out to God for forgiveness and found freedom. For the lost sheep, it was the Good Shepherd who went searching until He found it and carried it home on His shoulders (Luke 15:4–7).

Every story is unique, just as every child is unique. The way God reaches each wandering heart may be different, but His love is unchanging and His desire is always to bring them home. As Matthew says,

> So it is not the will of my Father who is in heaven that one of these little ones should perish.
>
> Matt 18:14 ESV

Today God is calling His prodigals into their inheritance!

Promises to Hold Onto!

(From the NIV, unless noted)

> The Lord will fight for you;
> you need only to be still.
>
> Ex 14:14

> The fruit of your womb will be blessed...
>
> Deut 28:4

> Those who sow with tears
> will reap with songs of joy.
>
> Ps 126:5

> Trust in the Lord with all your heart and lean not on your own understanding; in all your ways submit to him, and he will make your paths straight.
>
> Prov 3:5-6

> Train up a child in the way he should go;
> even when he is old he will not depart from it.
>
> Prov 22:6 ESV

But from everlasting to everlasting, the Lord's love is with those who fear him, and his righteousness with their children's children.

Ps 103: 17

...Blessed are those who fear the Lord, who find great delight in his commands. Their children will be mighty in the land; the generation of the upright will be blessed.

Ps 112: 1-2

Do not be afraid, for I am with you; I will bring your children from the east and gather you from the west. I will say to the north, 'Give them up!' and to the south, 'Do not hold them back.' Bring my sons from afar and my daughters from the ends of the earth.

Isa 43:5-6

...I will pour out my Spirit on your offspring, and my blessing on your descendants.

Isa 44:3

...I will contend with those who contend with you, and your children I will save.

Isa 49:25

See, I have written your name on the palms of my hands... Soon your descendants will come back, and all who are trying to destroy you will go away.

Isa 49:16-17 NLT

All your children will be taught by the Lord, and great will be their peace.

Isa 54:13

Surely the arm of the Lord is not too short to save, nor his ear too dull to hear.

Isa 59:1

... 'this is my covenant with them,' says the Lord: 'My Spirit that is upon you, and my words that I have put in your mouth, shall not depart out of your mouth, or out of the mouth of your offspring, or out of the mouth of your children's offspring,' says the Lord, 'from this time forth and forevermore.'

Isa 59:21 ESV

They will not work in vain, and their children will not be doomed to misfortune. For they are people blessed by the Lord, and their children, too, will be blessed.

Isa 65:23 NLT

...Restrain your voice from weeping and your eyes from tears, for your work will be rewarded, declares the Lord. They will return from the land of the enemy. So there is hope for your descendants,' declares the Lord. 'Your children will return to their own land.'

Jer 31:16-17

I am the Lord, the God of all mankind. Is anything too hard for me?

Jer 32:27

So I will restore to you the years that the swarming locust has eaten...

Joel 2:25 NKJV

My Father, who has given them to me, is greater than all; no one can snatch them out of my Father's hand.

Jn 10:29

Peter replied, 'Repent and be baptized, every one of you, in the name of Jesus Christ for the forgiveness of your sins. And you will receive the gift of the Holy Spirit. The promise is for you and your children and for all who are far off – for all whom the Lord our God will call.'

Acts 2:38-39

Christ Jesus who died—more than that, who was raised to life—is at the right hand of God and is also interceding for us.

Rom 8:34

Chapter 17

War over the Seed

As I was thinking about these women I am writing about in this book and the way they fought for the promise, I could see that from the first whisper of Eden's curse, there has been a war, not merely against women, but against what they carry. The seed. The promise. The redemption of the world. God declared that through the woman's offspring would come the One who would crush the serpent's head (Gen 3:15). And from that moment forward, the enemy set out to destroy the children born of promise. But generation after generation, God raised up women: broken, misunderstood, overlooked, and brought about His plan to bring Jesus into our world to save us. These women point to His grace.

Rachel: A Mother's Cry

> A voice is heard in Ramah, mourning and great weeping, Rachel weeping for her children, refusing to be comforted, because they are no more.

These words were first spoken in the context of the Babylonian exile in Jeremiah 31:15, when Israel's children were taken captive, torn from their homes, their land and their identity. Rachel, long dead, is portrayed poetically as weeping from her tomb in Bethlehem for the children of her descendants who were no more. It was a picture of deep, national sorrow.

These words echoed through time, finding their ultimate fulfilment at the birth of Jesus. When Herod, in a desperate grasp for power, ordered the slaughter of every male child under the age of two in Bethlehem (Matt 2:16-18), the tears of Rachel were heard again. She became the symbolic mother of Israel, grieving the loss of innocent lives in the face of satanic opposition to the Messiah's coming. But Rachel's tears are not the end of the story, for the next verse in Jeremiah promises restoration:

> 'There is hope for your future', says the Lord.
> 'Your children will come again to their own land.'
>
> Jer 31:17 NLT

Bathsheba: From Grief to Grace

Bathsheba's story is one of loss and redemption. She lost her first son to death, a painful consequence of David's sin. But in a surprising turn of grace, she bore another son, Solomon, meaning peace. And the Lord named him Jedidiah, meaning beloved of God. Her womb, touched by scandal and sorrow, brought forth peace and divine favour. Through her, the royal line of David continued unbroken. The enemy sought to destroy the plans God had for her, but God redeemed her fully.

Tamar: Fighting for Her Future

Tamar's boldness preserved a generation. Denied justice, she risked shame to ensure her father-in-law would fulfil his duty of providing offspring for her deceased husband. From that courageous act came twins, Perez and Zerah. '*Perez*', whose name means 'breakthrough',[1] would become part of the very lineage of Christ (Matt 1:3). Tamar's story is messy and complex, but her persistence made her a carrier of the covenant promise. She stood where no one else would and ensured the line did not die.

Ruth: The Outsider Redeemed

Ruth should have been cut off—a Moabitess, a widow, an outsider. Yet she clung to Naomi, declaring, 'Your God will be my God' (Ruth 1:16). Her faith and loyalty led her to Boaz and she stepped into the genealogy of Jesus. She gave birth to Obed, the grandfather of David. Had she not gone with Naomi, had she not gleaned in Boaz's field, the royal lineage would have lost a critical link. Ruth's womb, once barren and foreign, became a wellspring of inheritance.

Rahab: From Shame to Salvation

Rahab was a prostitute in Jericho, a city marked for destruction. But she believed. She hid the Israelite spies, declared allegiance to their God and tied the scarlet cord in her window as a sign of faith (Josh 2). Because of her faith, she and her household were saved. But more than that, Rahab married Salmon and gave birth to Boaz, yes, the same Boaz who would redeem Ruth (Matt 1:5). She was the least likely to be chosen, yet God brought her into the household of faith and placed her directly in the lineage of Jesus.

The Slaughter in Egypt: Moses Hidden

Centuries earlier, in Egypt, Pharaoh commanded the murder of every Hebrew male baby (Ex 1:15-22). But God saved Moses. He used a circle of courageous women to protect the promise: Hebrew midwives, who feared God more than Pharaoh, a mother who hid her son in faith, a sister who watched over him from the riverbank and even Pharaoh's own daughter, who drew him out of the water and raised him in the palace. Exodus 1:17 NIV says,

> The midwives, however, feared God and did not do what the king of Egypt had told them to do; they let the boys live.

Moses, the deliverer, was born under the shadow of genocide. The pattern repeats, wherever deliverance is about to be born, destruction tries to stop it. But God used women to keep the promise alive.

The War Against the Womb

Again and again, the enemy has made war against God's promises, especially those who were chosen to carry out God's purposes. From Tamar's scandal to Bathsheba's sorrow, from Rahab's reputation to Ruth's barrenness, these women overcame every attempt to disqualify them. They bore the lineage of the Messiah not because of perfection, but because of faith, courage and God's unfailing mercy.

Even Rachel's weeping was not without hope. Her tears speak for all mothers, those who have lost children, those who have been robbed of legacy and those who are still waiting to see a promise fulfilled. And God responds to Rachel's tears with this: 'Refrain your voice from weeping, and your eyes from tears... they shall come back from the land of the enemy.' (Jer 31:16 NKJV). The seed will not be lost. The inheritance will not be stolen.

It is the same today. Rachel's cry has become our own, the cry of mothers, grandmothers, sisters and intercessors for the children of this generation. Children lost to addiction, to confusion, to violence, to hopelessness. Family members who don't know Jesus, friends wandering far from their identity in Christ. There is a cry for them to be restored, to return. A cry not born of despair, but of hope, a cry God hears and answers.

Reflection: A Mother's Cry, A Generational Hope

We may not be living under the rule of Pharaoh or Herod, but the battle over children and generational legacy rages on. The enemy still wars against the seed, against hope, identity, purity, inheritance and promise. He targets the womb, the family and the future. But just like Rachel, Tamar, Bathsheba, Ruth, Rahab and so many others, we are women of the promise.

God still moves through women, through mothers, through tears, through hidden acts of bravery. He still writes legacy through women who believe, even when the odds are against them.

This is not just their story. It's ours. The Messiah came through a line of women who didn't give up. Now, we carry that same inheritance.

What promise or inheritance has God placed within you that is worth fighting for, weeping over and believing for?

The War Continues: Identity, Family and the Command to be Fruitful

Today, the war over the seed hasn't ended. What began as a war over children in Egypt and Bethlehem now plays out as a war over identity itself. It is a war on the family, on male and female and on the divine design God set in motion from the beginning.

God was the initiator of marriage. He created male and female in His image and He blessed them, saying,

> ...Be fruitful and multiply...
>
> Gen 1:28 NLT

That command to be fruitful was not just about physical reproduction, it was about legacy, identity and reflecting God's image on earth.

But now, the clarity of male and female is being intentionally blurred. Even in respected dictionaries, such as the Cambridge Dictionary, we now read definitions like:

> Man: An adult who lives and identifies as male, though they may have been considered to have a different sex at birth. [2]

This is more than cultural confusion; it is spiritual warfare. The enemy is still attacking the seed, but this time by undermining the very soil it grows in: identity, family, gender and the truth of God's Word.

We must recognise that our identity is not defined by culture, confusion or compromise. It is defined by Christ. The Word of God is our foundation and it speaks clearly and lovingly:

> So God created mankind in his own image, in the
> image of God he created them: male and female
> He created them.

Gen 1:27 NIV

There is no in-between, no blurring in God's design.

This battle is not just about politics or preference; it is about inheritance. It is about the command to be fruitful. If the enemy can distort identity, he can delay or even destroy destiny. But we are called to stand firm, to contend and believe for the restoration of what the enemy has tried to steal.

As The Passion Translation (a paraphrased version of the Bible) puts it so beautifully, you are His masterpiece!

> So God created man and woman and shaped
> them with his image inside them. In his own
> beautiful image, he created his masterpiece. Yes,
> male and female he created them. And God
> blessed them in his love, saying, 'Reproduce and
> be fruitful!...'

Gen 1:27-28

From the very beginning, God's blessing and purpose for humanity were tied to fruitfulness and His image in us – a promise that would ultimately be fulfilled in one Seed, Jesus Christ. This is why from Eden to Bethlehem and even to our day, the enemy has waged war against the seed – seeking to destroy what carries the promise, because the promise is found only in Jesus.

Jesus, the Promised Seed

In Galatians 3:16 NKJV we read,

> Now to Abraham and his Seed were the promises made. He does not say, 'And to seeds', as of many, but as of one, 'And to your Seed', who is Christ.

and in Galatians 3:28-29 NKJV it says:

> ...you are all one in Christ Jesus, and if you are Christ's then you are Abraham's seed and heirs according to the promise.

The promise to Abraham that he would be a father of many nations was fulfilled in Christ, who is the promise and the ultimate fulfilment of our lives. Through the cross, He became our Redeemer and our Father, and we become His children when we give our lives to Him, turn from our sin and make Him the Lord of our lives. Through faith and simply believing in Him, we can become children of God, and we are included in this promise. We become heirs of God's eternal promise! What an inheritance! He lives in us and we are in Him!

Part 5
Lineage of Grace

Chapter 18

From Walls to Legacy
Rahab

I would love to continue the story by looking at the beautiful women recorded in the genealogy of Jesus in Matthew chapter one. I don't know if you have ever looked into this, because just reading a long list who had who is not the average day's easy reading, but it sets the scene for the entrance of a King! 'It is important to Jewish people, because they were the proof of their identity and the rights to their inheritance.' [1]

Faith on the Wall

Rahab's story is recorded in Joshua 2 and 6, Hebrews 11:31 and James 2:25. Rahab is one of only two women named in Hebrews 11, the great 'Hall of Faith.' While she and Sarah couldn't be more different in background or social standing, what joins them is a shared legacy of faith. Sarah, the matriarch of Israel, received a miracle in her old age. Rahab, a Canaanite prostitute, risked everything on a God she had only heard stories about. But both women believed that faith changed their destiny.

Hebrews 11:31 NLT tells us,

> It was by faith that Rahab the prostitute was not destroyed with the people in her city who refused to obey God. For she had given a friendly welcome to the spies.

Rahab's story begins when Joshua secretly sends two spies into Jericho. The spies arrive at Rahab's house, a place of disrepute, yet divinely appointed. When the king of Jericho hears of their arrival, he sends messengers to demand that Rahab surrender the men. But in an act of courageous faith, Rahab hides the spies on her rooftop beneath stalks of flax. She sends the king's messengers away with a lie, claiming the men had already left.

Her decision was not random; it was a moment of revelation. She tells the spies:

> ...I know that the **Lord has given you this land...** For we have heard how the Lord dried up the water of the Red Sea for you when you came out of Egypt...**For the Lord your God, He *is* God in heaven above and on earth beneath.**
>
> Josh 2:9-11 NKJV

This Canaanite woman had a revelation! She had a revelation of what God would do for Israel and she also recognised the true God and believed in Him. It was personal for her!

Her plea for mercy wasn't just to save her life; it was an appeal for inheritance. She asked for kindness and protection for her entire family, showing not only faith but a heart for generational inheritance.

The spies agreed, giving her a sign:

> ...tie this cord of scarlet thread in the window through which you let us down...
>
> Josh 2:18 AMP

This crimson cord, hanging from her window on the city wall, became her sign of covenant, echoing the scarlet thread of redemption woven throughout Scripture. When Jericho fell, Rahab and her family were spared. Her home, built into the wall that collapsed, stood firm by God's design.

Rahab's faith was not passive but active, courageous and sacrificial. James affirms this, saying:

> ...was not even Rahab the prostitute considered righteous for what she did when she gave lodging to the spies and sent them off in a different direction?
>
> Jam 2:25 NIV

Faith that pleases God is faith that acts. As Hebrews 11:6 NIV reminds us,

> ...without faith it is impossible to please God...

Rahab's faith not only saved her, but it also brought her into the lineage of Christ. From a harlot in Jericho to a mother in Israel, she is named in the genealogy of Jesus. (Matt 1:5).

Rahab reminds us that faith has no prerequisites. God doesn't require a perfect past, only a heart willing to believe and obey.

The Crimson Cord of Courage

Rahab's story challenges us to consider where we've placed our trust. She lived on the edge, literally and spiritually. Her home on the wall of Jericho became the dividing line between destruction and deliverance. She could have clung to the security of her city, her past or her reputation, but instead, she reached for a new identity by faith.

Have you ever felt like your past disqualifies you from God's promises? Rahab proves that faith, not background, determines your future. The crimson cord in her window mirrors the blood of Jesus and is a shadow of His forgiveness poured out for our sins at the cross.

The human heart longs for refuge, safety and belonging. Rahab's window held a hidden beauty symbolising hope and the possibility of rescue. From her place on the wall, she watched the spies escape and waited for her own deliverance. That window became more than an opening; it became a visible sign of God's invitation into safety.

Centuries later, Song of Songs offers a similar picture: a Bridegroom draws near, watching and calling from outside the wall.

> Listen! My beloved! Look! Here he comes...
> Look! There he stands behind our wall, gazing
> through the windows, peering through the
> lattice. My beloved spoke and said to me, 'Arise,
> my darling, my beautiful one, come with me.'
>
> Song 2:8-10 NIV

Could it be that even then, behind Rahab's wall, her Beloved, God, was watching? The One who saw her heart before Jericho's fall, peering through the lattice, was already pursuing her?

Jesus shows this same tender pursuit when He says:

> Behold, I stand at the door and knock. If anyone
> hears my voice and opens the door, I will come in
> to him and dine with him, and he with Me.
>
> Rev 3:20 NKJV

Rahab's window, the Bridegroom's call and Jesus' words in Revelation all share a central message. God actively seeks His people, offering safety, love and belonging, and inviting them into a personal relationship with Him.

Rahab opened the door of her heart long before her city's walls fell. She responded to God's call. Her faith brought salvation to her entire household and she entered Jesus' lineage.

Rahab reminds us that revelation comes to unexpected people in unexpected places. When God stirs your heart, will you respond? Will you believe He has a place for you?

May we, like Rahab, declare:

> ...for the Lord your God, he is God in the heavens above and on the earth beneath.
>
> Josh 2:11 ESV

May we live with the scarlet thread of redemption always visible, testifying to the faith that saves and the God who redeems.

Reflection

What walls have you lived behind that God is inviting you to step out from?

Where is He asking you to act courageously in faith?

Could this be the start of salvation coming to your household?

Chapter 19

Justice in the Shadow of Shame

Tamar

Tamar's story is not one we often teach in Sunday school. It's uncomfortable, raw, even scandalous. Tamar's story is recorded in Genesis 38.

She married into the family of Judah, who was one of the twelve sons of Jacob. She became the wife of Er, Judah's firstborn. But Er was wicked in the sight of the Lord and he died (Gen 38:7). As was the custom in those days, Tamar was given to the second brother, Onan, so that he might raise up an heir in his brother's name. Yet Onan refused to give her a child and refused to extend inheritance to her, because he knew the child would not be counted as his. And God saw his injustice and he also died.

Tamar, now twice widowed and still childless, was promised the youngest brother, Shelah, once he came of age. But Judah withheld Shelah, afraid that he too might die. He saw the pattern of death but did not see his own responsibility. Tamar was left waiting, wearing widow's garments, trapped in a system that had no intention of setting her free.

However, Tamar was not passive in the face of these challenges.

When the time came, she removed her widow's garments, veiled herself and took her stand beside the road where Judah was travelling. He did not recognise her, only saw a veiled woman by the wayside. In his hypocrisy, he desired her and she agreed on one condition. As a pledge, she asked for his signet ring, his cord and his staff. These represented his identity, his authority and his promise.

When Tamar's pregnancy became known, Judah was quick to accuse.

> ...Bring her out and have her burned to death!
>
> Gen 38:24 NIV

But Tamar sent the signet, the cord and the staff with a simple message:

> ...I am pregnant by the man who owns these..
> see if you recognise whose seal and cord and staff these are.
>
> Gen 38:25 NIV

In that moment, the tables turned. Judah's own unrighteousness was revealed and he confessed,

> ...She is more righteous than I, since I wouldn't give her to my son Shelah...
>
> Gen 38:26 NIV

Tamar gave birth to twins. During the birth, one child, Zerah, extended his hand first and the midwife tied a scarlet cord around it. The scarlet cord was wrapped around his hand to indicate that he was the firstborn and the one to receive the inheritance; however, Perez was born first! *'Perez'*, whose name means 'breakthrough', was born first. [1]

This was no ordinary child. Perez became the forefather of King David and generations later, of Jesus Christ, the Redeemer. Tamar, a Canaanite woman, cast aside by the system, became a cornerstone in the lineage of the Messiah.

She didn't just fight for herself, but she secured an inheritance for generations to come.

This act of divine reversal reveals a spiritual truth: God does not always honour man's systems or expectations. He often brings about redemption in ways that run counter to our expectations.

The Scarlet Thread of Redemption

We often hear about the scarlet cord in the story of Rahab; however, when I looked at these beautiful women, a pattern emerged. A thread of scarlet running through their stories and through ours today.

The scarlet cord we saw in Rahab's story as a symbol of protection and redemption is repeated in the story of Tamar, where a scarlet thread was tied around Zerah's hand at birth, marking his claim to inheritance and identity. But we also see God's sovereign intervention in this story.

These scarlet cords, one around a baby's wrist and one hanging from a harlot's window, are not coincidences. They echo a divine pattern:

The scarlet cord marks who is chosen, but God can reverse the order as He did with Perez. The scarlet cord marks those who are redeemed, even if they come from the margins like Rahab. The scarlet cord points to Christ, whose blood becomes the ultimate mark of redemption, inheritance and salvation.

Scarlet appears again and again in the Bible. Not just in Rahab's window, but in places of sacrifice and worship. We also see in Exodus 26:1 and 28:6 where the scarlet thread is used in the tabernacle and in the priestly garments. Scarlet points to sacrifice, redemption, grace and the blood of Jesus shed for us at the cross.

Isaiah talks about this image of scarlet to describe our sin and God's forgiveness:

> ...Though your sins are like scarlet,
> they shall be as white as snow:

> though they are red like crimson,
> They shall be as wool.
>
> Isa 1:18 NKJV

You may have 'though' in your story. Though you were overlooked. Though you made mistakes. Though you carry shame. Though you have sinned...

'Though' doesn't speak over your life. The cross has the final word and His blood speaks a better word!

You are forgiven! You are redeemed! You are free! There is no more condemnation!

You have an inheritance in Christ!

Even before He went to the cross, they dressed Him in a scarlet robe (Matt 27:28), declaring to the world that this blood is for you! The Romans put it on him and mocked him, but little did they know the significance of this robe.

You may feel cast aside, marked by sin, shame, unseen like Tamar, rejected like Hagar or an outsider like Rahab, but His blood is for you. The Cross is enough!

Identity, Authority and Ownership

As I was reading this story of Tamar, I was reflecting on the importance of the items she took from Judah and what they mean for us today. How do they reflect our inheritance?

When Tamar disguised herself and met Judah on the road, she asked for:

- His signet ring

- His cord (or bracelet)

- His staff

Each of these items carried deep personal and symbolic meaning. Tamar was asking for proof of his identity, authority and ownership. And prophetically, these objects speak to us about who we are in Christ.

Let's look at each one.

The Signet Ring – Identity and Authority

In ancient times, a signet ring was like a signature. It had the family seal carved into it and was used to stamp documents, authorise decrees and prove legal ownership.

By keeping Judah's signet ring, Tamar held onto a piece of his identity and legal authority. It was irrefutable proof of who he was and of what he had done.

In Scripture, the signet ring represents identity and royal authority!

> ...I will make you like my signet ring, for I have chosen you...
>
> Hag 2:23 NIV

> Set me as a seal upon your heart, as a seal upon your arm, for love is strong as death, jealousy is fierce as the grave. Its flashes are flashes of fire, the very flame of the Lord.
>
> Song 8:6 ESV

> Now write another decree in the king's name... and seal it with the king's signet ring – for no document written in the king's name and sealed with his ring can be revoked.
>
> Est 8:8 NIV

> When you believed, you were marked in Him with a seal, the promised Holy Spirit, who is a deposit guaranteeing our inheritance ...
>
> Eph 1:13-14 NIV

When we come to Jesus, we are given a new identity. We are no longer defined by our past, our shame or our thoughts. We are sealed as daughters of God, chosen and marked by His Spirit.

Our Identity

Here are just some reminders of your identity in Christ. (NIV)

I am loved.

> I have loved you with an everlasting love; I have drawn you with unfailing kindness.
>
> Jer 31:3

I am accepted.

> To the praise of the glory of His grace, by which He made us accepted in the Beloved.
>
> Eph 1:6 NKJV

I am valued.

> You were bought at a price...
>
> 1 Cor 6:20

I belong.

> Now you are the body of Christ, and each one of
> you is a part of it.
>
> 1 Cor 12:27

The Cord – A Binding Covenant

'In the ancient Near Eastern context, a cord could be used to secure the seal, often worn around the neck or wrist. The cord's inclusion in the pledge to Tamar highlights its role as an integral part of the seal's function, ensuring it was kept close to the owner and readily available for use.' The cord, therefore, represents the intimacy, identity and nearness of the one who wore it. In giving Tamar his cord, Judah unknowingly offered Tamar a piece of his everyday life and himself. [2]

The symbolism of this cord speaks to intimacy, identity, connection, covenant and a binding promise – all of which echo powerfully in our own relationship with Christ.

This points to the covenant God has made with us through Jesus. We are bound to Him, covered in His righteousness, no longer separated. The cord reminds us that our salvation is not based on what we do, but on what Christ has done.

Now pause and see the thread that runs between Tamar's cord and Zerah's cord:

> Tamar held a cord of promise, evidence of her right to inheritance through Judah.
>
> Her son Zerah bore a cord of inheritance, but it was Perez, the unmarked one, who actually received it.

This is a picture of how God's inheritance comes, not always through human order or tradition, but through God's sovereign will.

It's also a picture of Jesus. Just as Perez carried the lineage that would lead to King David and Christ, we too inherit, not because of position or works, but because of the grace and sovereignty of God.

It was at the cross that there was a great exchange – Jesus clothed us in His righteousness and broke through on our behalf so we can now break through into the inheritance that Christ has for us.

The Staff – Authority and Shepherding

When Tamar took Judah's staff, she wasn't just holding a stick. She held onto his authority, his responsibility, his role as the leader of the family line. As she claimed this staff, she was claiming her inheritance.

A staff was more than just a walking stick. It symbolised leadership and protection. Leaders used it as a sign of their role and responsibility.

Moses was one such leader who used a staff to perform miracles, symbolising divine authority, such as in Exodus 4. He also used a staff to split the seas. (Ex 14:16)

Shepherds used it to guide and protect their flocks. Here in Psalm 23, the staff is described.

> ...Your rod [to protect] and Your staff [to guide], they comfort and console me.
>
> Ps 23:4 AMP

The staff points to Jesus as our Good Shepherd and to the authority He gives to us as His followers. He leads, protects and sends us out with His name and authority. It also speaks of the call to walk uprightly, leaning not on our own strength, but on His.

When we come into Christ, we receive His commission. We are seated with Him, given His name and walk in His power to fulfil the calling He has on our lives.

> And God raised us up with Christ and seated us with Him in the heavenly realms in Christ Jesus.
>
> Eph 2:6 NIV

> I have given you authority... to overcome all the power of the enemy; nothing will harm you.
>
> Luke 10:19 NIV

> All authority in heaven and on earth has been given to Me. Therefore, go and make disciples of all nations, baptizing them in the name of the Father and of the Son and of the Holy Spirit,
>
> Matt 28:18-19 NIV

You don't stand in your own strength, you stand in His Name, His authority, His Spirit and His Word!

Reflection

Perez, Tamar's son, means 'breakthrough'. Are you praying for a breakthrough in any area?

How might your story become part of someone else's breakthrough?

Tamar held on to Judah's staff, signet and cord, which were symbols of identity, authority and promise. What are you holding onto?

Chapter 20
Crowned in Grace
Bathsheba

Daughter of Abundance

Bathsheba's name means 'daughter of abundance'. [1] What a powerful name! Her story is found in 2 Samuel 11-12 and 1 Kings 1. At first glance, her story might seem anything but abundant. She enters Scripture as the wife of a brave and loyal man named Uriah. Even in the genealogy recorded in Matthew, she is referred to as 'the wife of Uriah' (Matt 1:6). I find that fascinating! I think that this is to remind us of her story of restoration and how God redeemed the brokenness of her life.

One day, King David saw Bathsheba from the rooftop, desired her and asked for her. From that encounter, she became pregnant. So much shame! David tried to cover his sin and called Uriah home from battle, offering him food and wine and urging him to sleep with his wife so that the child could be passed off as his. But Uriah, a man of integrity, refused to enjoy comforts at home while his fellow soldiers remained at war and refused to go home to his wife.

So this plan failed and David came up with a darker scheme. He wrote to Joab, the army commander, instructing him to place Uriah on the front lines,

> ...where the fighting is fiercest. Then withdraw from him so that he will be struck down and die.
>
> 2 Sam 11:15 NIV

The plan succeeded and Uriah was killed in battle. After a period of mourning, David married Bathsheba.

What a tragic twist in the story of a man described as '*after God's own heart*' (Acts 13:22). It raises deep questions about how Bathsheba felt. I wonder if she was even aware of David's murder of her husband? I wonder what her response would have been.

God did not overlook David's sin. He sent the prophet Nathan to confront him with a parable and David, upon hearing it, unwittingly condemned himself. Through this parable, Nathan revealed David's guilt. In response, David penned Psalm 51, a deep cry of repentance:

> Create in me a pure heart, O God, and renew a right spirit within me.
>
> Ps 51:10 ESV

Yet the consequences of his sin remained. The child born from the union with Bathsheba became ill and died. David fasted and prayed, but when the child passed, he rose, worshipped and accepted the Lord's judgment. Bathsheba, herself, must have been experiencing such deep grief after the loss of her husband and now her child.

But the story doesn't end there.

Bathsheba bore another son named *'Solomon'*, meaning peaceful. [2] Nathan also prophesied over this child, naming him Jedidiah!

> ...The Lord loved him; and because the Lord loved him, he sent word through Nathan the prophet to name him Jedidiah.
>
> 2 Sam 12:24-25 NIV

'Jedidiah' means 'beloved by the Lord'. [3] Solomon, the son of a deeply broken situation, was chosen and cherished.

Bathsheba's story is a stunning picture of both pain and redemption. She witnessed the depths of human failure but also the restorative hand of God. Through her came a king and ultimately, through her lineage, Jesus, the Messiah.

Bathsheba's name, daughter of abundance, seemed to contrast with her early experiences. Her story began in the shadow of betrayal, grief and national scandal, but it did not end there. God, in His mercy, rewrote her legacy. Though drawn into the sin of a king and marked by the death of a child, Bathsheba emerges not as a discarded woman but as the mother of King Solomon and a woman included in the lineage of Jesus (Matt 1:6). Her name is not erased. Grace became part of Bathsheba's story. It didn't make sense, but God stepped into her world and offered what no one else could. That is inheritance.

Like Bathsheba, many women have known what it is to be used, misjudged or dismissed. Yet the story of Bathsheba reveals that God doesn't discard the broken; He lifts them into legacy. She became the mother of a king and a woman who saw the promise of peace (Solomon) born from a place of pain.

In Bathsheba, we see that inheritance is not always given in perfect circumstances. Sometimes, it's born through heartbreak, injustice and scandal. Yet God, in His sovereignty, transforms what the enemy meant for evil and repositions us for destiny.

Her life declares: 'Your past does not disqualify you from inheritance, but God can crown you in the very place where you were once covered in shame.'

Re-positioned to Reign: A Royal Inheritance

Just like Bathsheba, we have been re-positioned by grace. Through Jesus Christ, we are no longer defined by failure, shame or the labels others have given us. He declares over us that we are:

> ...a chosen people, a royal priesthood, a holy nation, God's special possession, that you may declare the praises of Him who called you out of darkness into His wonderful light.
>
> 1 Pet 2:9 NIV

We have been seated in heavenly places with Christ (Eph 2:6), crowned with righteousness and made co-heirs with Him. Our past has been redeemed and our future is secure in His hands. This is the inheritance of sons and daughters.

From Wounded to Victorious

The song *I'm No Victim* by Kristine Di Marco has powerful words that declare that we are fully loved, covered by His love, adopted into God's family and living with a vision. [4] He is our Father with good plans for our lives. His Word defines who we are and our true home is with the King!

We are very much loved by God and daughters of the King! We can live with a future that is not defined by our past. Bathsheba could have remained in a cycle of victim mentality, living under the weight of her past and her brokenness, but she walked into the very plans and purposes that God had for her life.

> A victim mentality is a persistent and often harmful mindset where people view themselves as powerless and constantly wronged by others or by their circumstances... it's a learned behaviour

formed when people believe they lack control over their lives. [5]

There is no denying that Bathsheba experienced real suffering; however, she could have remained in the shadows, quietly grieving, but the mercy of God repositioned her and brought her into her true identity as the mother of a king and a daughter of abundance. She was transformed through grace, as God healed her heart and although she was a victim of her circumstances, her identity was not defined by what had happened to her. She was restored and learnt to trust God with her heart.

That is the difference between a person living in a victim mentality and a person living in victory. A victor rises by the power of what Christ has done for them in spite of what has been done to them. A victim does not need to be defined by their past, pain, betrayal, injustice or failure, BUT as a victor, they can be defined by their position. We are seated with Christ, clothed in righteousness and heirs of His Kingdom. A victim may say: 'This is just who I am. I'll always be stuck here', BUT a victor knows: 'I am who He says I am, I am more than a conqueror, I have been chosen, adopted, loved and crowned with grace.' Living in victory declares that the wrong done does NOT have the final word! It is not pretending the pain never happened, but it is allowing God to heal the broken pieces and restore purpose to your life. Psalm 147:3 TPT paraphrase declares:

He heals the wounds of every shattered heart.

The Kingdom of God is not built on perfect stories. It's built on redeemed ones. In Christ, you are a royal heir. You carry purpose, authority and inheritance.

> ...in all these things we are more than conquerors through Him who loved us.
>
> Rom 8:37 NIV

Like Bathsheba, even if your story began in pain, God is writing your story, a story of redemption and grace. He is crowning you in the very place you were once crushed. You are not what happened to you - you are who He says you are.

Crowned in Beauty

Bathsheba's life is a testimony that God can restore the broken, redeem the fallen and reposition the overlooked for eternal purpose. She was once known only as 'the wife of Uriah', a woman caught in the shadows of a king's failure, but God crowned her with beauty, lifted her in honour and placed her in the royal lineage of the Messiah.

He still does the same today. These are some beautiful promises for His precious daughters today!

> ...to bestow on them a crown of beauty
> instead of ashes,
> the oil of joy instead of mourning,

and a garment of praise
instead of a spirit of despair...

Isa 61:3 NIV

You will be a crown of splendour in the Lord's hand, a royal diadem in the hand of your God.

Isa 62:3 NIV

You are crowned with beauty, clothed with righteousness and seated with Christ in heavenly places. Like Bathsheba, your life is a portrait of His redemptive story, a story of inheritance found in Christ.

Reflection

What does it mean to you to be seated with Christ in heavenly places?

How might your perspective change if you lived daily from that position of victory? Do you see yourself the way God sees you? Crowned in beauty, chosen and dearly loved?

What might be holding you back from fully embracing this truth?

Chapter 21

Carrying the Promise of Heaven

Mary

Inheritance No Matter Your Age

Mary was young. Some say barely more than a girl when the angel of the Lord came to her. Unmarried, unseen by the world, tucked away in a small town with no special status, but seen by God. And chosen. Her story is found in Matthew 1-2 and Luke 1-2.

Her story reminds us that inheritance in the Kingdom of God is not about age, status or stage of life. It's about the heart that says yes. When heaven spoke, Mary didn't argue. She surrendered, even in her fear:

> ...Let it be unto me according to your word.
>
> Lk 1:38 NKJV

Though young and likely misunderstood, Mary carried the promise. And she didn't just carry it physically—she carried it in her heart. When she visited Elizabeth, she erupted in a song of praise. That song echoed the words of another woman of inheritance: Hannah. Two women generations apart, both overlooked by others, but both honoured by God. Hannah's journey can be found in 1 Samuel 1:2-2:21.

So wherever you are, young or old, waiting or wondering, don't let go of the Word He has spoken to you. Mary 'treasured up all these things and pondered them in her heart' (Lk 2:19 NIV). She didn't broadcast every detail, but she held tight to the promise. That's your invitation too.

Hold onto what He has spoken over your life. Don't let your age, delay or your circumstances define your destiny. Your inheritance is secure, not because of who you are, but because of who He is.

His Word will not return void. So rest. Wait. Worship. And like Mary, sing while you carry the promise.

Prophetic Mothers of Inheritance

Hannah and Mary are like mirror reflections across the Old and New Testaments – two women, two songs, one heart of worship. I love exploring both their similarities and differences, their circumstances, their responses and their posture before God. Each sang from a place of deep surrender and humility and their worship continues to bless generations. (Hannah's song is found in 1 Sam 2:1-10; Mary's song is in Luke 1:46-55 NIV) Similar verses from each of their songs are compared below:

Hannah: My heart rejoices in the Lord; in the Lord my horn is lifted high... (2)
Mary: ...My soul glorifies the Lord, and my spirit rejoices in God my Savior. (46-47)

Hannah: There is no one holy like the Lord; there is no one besides you; there is no Rock like our God. (2)
Mary: For the Mighty One has done great things for me—holy is his name. (49)

Hannah: Those who were full hire themselves out for food, but those who were hungry are hungry no more. (5)
Mary: He has filled the hungry with good things but has sent the rich away empty. (53)

Hannah: He raises the poor from the dust and lifts the needy from the ash heap; he seats them with princes and has them inherit a throne of honour. (8)
Mary: He has brought down rulers from their thrones but has lifted up the humble. (52)

> **Hannah**: He will give strength to his king and exalt the horn of his anointed." (10)
> **Mary**: He has helped his servant Israel, remembering to be merciful to Abraham and his descendants forever... (54-55)

Both of these songs are profoundly prophetic. Both Hannah and Mary declare divine truths that reach far beyond their own lives. Their words reveal God's heart for the lowly, the poor, the humble and the hungry, for those the world often overlooks. From places of deep vulnerability, they worship with hearts bowed in humility. They rejoiced in God, allowing worship to rise from them as they made space in their hearts to receive and release what God was pouring out.

There are clear differences between these two women. Initially, Hannah was barren and mocked, carrying the weight of unanswered prayers and public shame; Mary was young, unmarried and lived without status or influence. Hannah worshipped *after* receiving her promise, after Samuel was born. Mary worshipped *before* her promise was fulfilled and Jesus had not been born, yet she lifted her voice in faith in Elizabeth's home after Elizabeth said to her,

> Blessed is she who has believed that the Lord would fulfil his promises to her!
>
> Lk 1:45 NIV

Hannah sang in the temple after giving her son back to the Lord. She worshipped from a place of sacrifice. Mary sang while still carrying the promise within her. She worshipped from a place of faith. Hannah lived during a time of spiritual dryness and instability, in the era of the Judges. Mary, by contrast, lived under Roman occupation, in an age when many longed for a military Messiah to establish an earthly kingdom.

Though their stories span generations, their surrender and songs reveal a shared inheritance of trust, courage and divine calling. Each woman worshipped not because everything made sense, but because they believed in the faithfulness of the One who had spoken. They knew God was sovereign.

Despite different seasons, both women found their identity and inheritance in God's faithfulness.

Worship is your Inheritance too

There is a deep relationship between sacrifice and singing. Worship is often birthed out of surrender. Sometimes we sing in faith until our hearts yield. Other times, like Hannah, we walk in obedience and sacrifice, then we sing. Hannah gave Samuel back to God, the very answer to her prayers. Out of that place of surrender, her song rose in thanksgiving.

Samuel himself was a child of promise, as Jesus was. Both were born through divine intervention, dedicated fully to God and raised up for a holy purpose. Samuel became a prophet and priest. Jesus is our prophet, priest and king. Hannah's prayer was more than a personal song; it was a prophetic declaration. It pointed to the future anointing of

King David, but also symbolically foreshadowed Jesus, the Anointed One who would bring salvation to the world.

Samuel was a deliverer of Israel in his time. Jesus is the eternal Deliverer for all humanity. The parallels between these two promised sons deepen the beauty and significance of the songs that came before them.

This connection is especially meaningful to me because my daughter's name is Hannah. Her name, like Hannah's prayer, speaks of grace. When I read Hannah's song, I see the goodness of God in her life and in my daughter's life, too.

Worship is not just a response to blessing. It is part of the inheritance itself. Hannah and Mary gave voice to the greatness of God and their words became eternal. Worship affirms who God is and that He alone is sovereign. Even in uncertainty, worshipping God anchors us in a firm foundation. Worship is prophetic and helps to see what heaven sees over our lives, even when the circumstances aren't lining up.

Whether you are young or old, barren or expectant, worship while you wait. Let praise be the stone in your hand and the spring in your soul.

The verse that touches me most deeply is this one:

> He raises the poor from the dust
> and lifts the needy from the ash heap;
> he seats them with princes

> and has them inherit a throne of
> honour.

1 Sam 2:8 NIV

This is the heart of God to bring restoration to those in need. This verse speaks into countless lives around the world, where we glimpse the beginnings of divine exchange, beauty for ashes and an unfolding story of restoration.

Reflection

What part of Mary or Hannah's song resonates with you?

How is worship your inheritance?

What promise from God are you pondering in your heart?

Chapter 22

Harvesting what she didn't Sow

Ruth

From Famine to Fullness

We find Ruth's story in Ruth 1-4. In the days when the judges ruled, a famine struck the land of Judah. In search of survival, a man named Elimelech took his wife Naomi and their two sons, Mahlon and Chilion, to live in the country of Moab. But there, tragedy struck. First, Elimelech died. Then both sons passed away, leaving Naomi and her two daughters-in-law, Ruth and Orpah, widowed and weary.

'Chilion', whose name means 'fragility or consumption', and *'Mahlon'*, meaning 'sickness or weakness', carried names that spoke of decline and loss. Ruth had been married into a story marked by sickness, yet her own name spoke of a different future. *'Ruth'* means 'friend or companion.'[1] She was destined for something more.

When Naomi decided to return to *'Bethlehem'*, meaning the 'House of Bread', [2] she urged her daughters-in-law to stay in Moab. Orpah kissed her and stayed behind, but Ruth clung to her with covenant love and fierce loyalty. Her response still echoes today:

> ...Don't urge me to leave you or to turn back from you. Where you go I will go, and where you stay I will stay. Your people will be my people, and your God my God. Where you die I will die, and there I will be buried. May the Lord deal with me, be it ever so severely, if even death separates you and me.
>
> Ruth 1:16–17 NIV

So the two women journeyed back to Bethlehem, where the famine had ended and the harvest had begun. What began in sorrow and despair was giving way to joy and delight. Famine would soon become harvest.

Together, they returned to Bethlehem, where the barley harvest was beginning, a season of new life, hope and plenty.

Here, in the fields, Ruth gleaned the leftover grain. This was the grain that others had missed or dropped. She walked behind the harvesters, gathering the fragments, much like a seed resting beneath the soil, hidden, vulnerable, but destined for growth.

Jesus said:

> ...unless a grain of wheat falls into the earth and dies, it remains alone; but if it dies, it bears much fruit.
>
> John 12:24 ESV

Ruth had walked through a season of poverty, grief and heartache. Everything familiar had died – her husband, her home and her identity. It was a burial of what once was. But in God's hands, even the burial of the old becomes the planting of something new. From her emptiness came a deeper filling. The pouring out of loss made room for God to pour in purpose, inheritance and a new season. Ruth's story reminds us that our lowest valleys can become the very soil where new life takes root. What feels like the end is often just the beginning in the beautiful plans that God has for our lives.

In those fields, Ruth met Boaz, a man of strength and tenderness. Ruth found grace. Gleaning behind the reapers, gathering the leftover grain, she was seen. Boaz noticed her, not just her beauty, but her faithfulness, humility and courage. Boaz was a man of strength, but also of tenderness. He protected Ruth, blessed her and eventually fulfilled the role of *kinsman-redeemer*.

The role of a kinsman-redeemer is that of a close relative with the responsibility and honour to redeem a widow and preserve the family line. Boaz showed generosity and faithfulness, going beyond the expectations of the law to provide for Ruth.

And in Boaz, we see a man as tender as the woman he redeems. He reflects the heart of Christ Himself, strong yet kind.

Ruth, a Gentile woman, married a Jewish man and became the great-grandmother of King David—an ancestor of Jesus, the Messiah. Her story foreshadows God's plan to include the outsider, the foreigner and the forgotten into His family.

Boaz and Ruth then had a son named Obed. Obed became the father of Jesse. Jesse became the father of David. And through David's royal line, Jesus, our eternal Redeemer, came.

Ruth's story reminds us that nothing is wasted in God's hands. Grief becomes grace. Loss becomes legacy. And empty fields, when walked with faith, become a plentiful harvest.

The Redeemer's Grace

Ruth had nothing. She was a widow, poor and a foreigner—an outsider with no rights, no inheritance and no reason to expect kindness in a new land. She had no status! All she could do was gather the leftover grain and according to the law of Israel, the poor were allowed to glean behind the reapers. It was a mercy written into the law, but it still left Ruth at the bottom. She was gathering crumbs. No position, no provision and no promise...yet.

But in came Boaz.

Boaz saw her. He noticed her hard work, her dignity and her devotion to Naomi. But more than that, Boaz was moved by compassion. He told the harvesters to leave extra grain behind for her. He offered her protection, favour and eventually his hand in marriage. Boaz wasn't obligated, but he chose her. Boaz is a beautiful picture of Jesus, our Kinsman-Redeemer.

Where Ruth could only collect scraps, Boaz gave her abundance. Where she had no right to belong, he gave her a place at his table. Where she had no future, he gave her a destiny.

> He has brought me to his banqueting table, and
> his banner over me is love...
>
> Song 2:4 AMP

Jesus, like Boaz, steps into our brokenness. He finds us in the dust of our desperation and He doesn't just leave us there. He calls us by name. He invites us in. He provides more than we ever asked or imagined. He gives us good things, not because we've earned them, but because He delights in redeeming us. This act of redemption is a beautiful picture of what Jesus did for us.

Ruth went from gleaning leftovers to becoming his bride. From picking up scattered grain to holding her own child in her arms. From stranger to family. From outsider to ancestor of the Messiah.

That is the grace of our God. And like Ruth, we may come to Him empty, but we never leave the same.

The Full Price — A Picture of Jesus' Sacrifice

Boaz didn't just offer kindness to Ruth; he paid the full price to redeem her. In the culture and law of Israel, a kinsman-redeemer had the right and the responsibility to buy back a relative's property or marry a widow to preserve the family line. Boaz willingly took on this role and made the full payment, securing Ruth's place, her dignity and her future.

This act of redemption is a beautiful picture of what Jesus did for us.

Just like Boaz, Jesus paid the full price for our redemption. We were lost, without rights and powerless to save ourselves. But God loved us so much that He sent His Son as the perfect sacrifice. Jesus became the spotless Lamb, the ransom for our sins.

> For the wages of sin is death, but the gift of God is eternal life in Christ Jesus our Lord.
>
> Rom 6:23 NIV

Boaz's faithful love and integrity brought blessing, not only to Ruth but to the generations that followed. Likewise, Jesus' faithfulness to the Father and to us secured our eternal blessing.

God paid the price; Jesus gave His life so we could be redeemed and bought back from death, shame and separation. Just as Boaz's payment restored Ruth's hope and inheritance, Jesus' sacrifice restores our relationship with God and secures for us eternal life.

Ruth's story beautifully points us to the Gospel: we were once without hope, but because of Jesus, the ultimate Kinsman-Redeemer, we are now heirs with Christ.

Shelter Under His Wings

Ruth's story is a vivid picture of God's faithfulness and redemption and how He brings new life and shelter through seasons of loss, pressing and waiting.

In Ruth chapter 2 verse 12 NIV, Boaz speaks a blessing over Ruth:

> May the Lord repay you for what you have done. May you be richly rewarded by the Lord, the God of Israel, under whose **wings** you have come to take refuge.

The Hebrew word used here is *'kanaph'*, meaning 'wings'[3] and is a beautiful image of God's protective, sheltering love. Just as birds cover their young with their wings to protect and nurture them, God lovingly shelters His people.[4]

Later, in Ruth chapter 3 verse 9 NIV, Ruth courageously approaches Boaz and says:

> ...Spread the **corner of your garment** over me, since you are a guardian-redeemer of our family."

The 'corner of the garment' is also called *'kanaph'*, the same word for 'wing'. This refers to the literal corner or edge of a cloak or robe that could be wrapped around someone. In Hebrew culture, when a man spread the corner of his garment over a woman, it symbolised taking her under his protection and taking her as his wife.[5]

Ruth's appeal to Boaz was more than a request for protection; it was a plea for covenant care and security. Boaz responded by accepting that role, pledging to redeem and marry her.

This tender image of finding shelter under the wings of a Redeemer connects deeply to God's heart for us. Throughout Scripture, God invites us to take refuge under His wings, offering shelter, safety and care in every season.

A Story of Redemption and New Life

Ruth's story is not only about protection and shelter but also about new life emerging from hardship and pressing like grapes crushed in a wine press to produce new wine, or a seed dying in the soil to bring forth an abundant harvest.

Ruth's humble gleaning among the leftover grain in Boaz's field was the beginning of God's harvest season—bringing blessing and legacy from what seemed small and discarded.

Boaz's faithful redemption mirrors Jesus, who paid the full price for our salvation, taking us under His protective wings and inviting us into His family.

Reflection

Are there areas in your life, past or present, that feel broken, empty or in need of God's redemption and restoration? Could this be the beginning of a new season He is inviting you into?

Have you made room for God to pour into you and fill you with His presence, peace and purpose?

Have you allowed yourself to rest under His wings and to truly believe that you are redeemed, valued and bought with a price? What does it look like for you to take shelter in God's love like Ruth did with Boaz, to come under His covering, protection and covenant promise?

Part 6
Your Invitation!

Chapter 23
Invitation to the Springs
Receiving your Inheritance

You are His Beloved Child!

There is an inheritance beyond earthly value. It is spiritual and eternal, flowing like a quiet stream from God's heart into ours! Your inheritance is not only what you receive, but also understanding how precious you are to God. Psalm 139 reminds us that,

> Your eyes saw my unformed body; all the days ordained for me were written in your book...
>
> Ps 139:16 NIV

Before anyone else placed value on you, God knew your name and called you His own.

To receive your inheritance is to rest in knowing that Jesus is the author of your story. He loves you and you are beautiful to Him!

> You are known.
> You are seen.
> You are loved.
> You are valued.
> You belong.
> Your heart has a home in God.

This was the testimony of Judith, my beautiful friend saved out of witchcraft, who made Jesus the centre of her life. She didn't complicate it. She simply believed and turned from her sin. She believed that Jesus had given His life for her on the cross and her heart became a home for Christ when she surrendered her life to Him and made Him the Lord of her life. And in that place, she discovered an inheritance that had been waiting for her all along.

> Anyone who believes in Me may come and drink!
> For the Scriptures declare, 'Rivers of living water
> will flow from his heart.'
>
> John 7:38 NLT

The inheritance God has for you is not just truth to understand or promises to remember. It's the power to receive His living, overflowing presence inside you. That presence is the Holy Spirit. Jesus spoke of Him as 'rivers of living water' that would flow from the depths of those who believed in Him. On the Day of Pentecost, this promise became reality: ordinary men and women were filled with the Holy Spirit and they began to speak in new languages, declaring the wonders of God (Acts 2:1–4). This wasn't just for them. It's for you. It's for today.

> This promise is for you and your children and for all who are far off, for all whom the Lord our God will call.
>
> Acts 2:39 NIV

If you are thirsty, ask for more of God, more of His life and more of His power. Just like Achsah, who asked for water and Hagar, who lifted up her voice, look to Him today.

Just come in simple faith, surrender your heart and receive. And the living water will flow, not just for you, but for others. Your family. Your friends. Your generation. This is your inheritance.

> ...Be filled with the Spirit...
>
> Eph 5:18 NIV

Precious Promises

My grandma had a beautiful habit of marking in the margins of her Bible any revelation from God's Word that deeply touched her heart with the letters 'PP' . Sometimes she'd include a date alongside them. 'PP' stood for 'precious promises'. These weren't just underlined verses; they were wells of life. Springs in the desert. Moments when the Living Word pierced her heart and stirred something eternal within her. They became anchors of faith, words she learned to stand on, believe in and hold fast to until they came to pass.

These revelations became her spiritual heirlooms. They didn't die with her; they continue to flow. To my mother. To me. To my children. And now, to you.

That's what inheritance looks like in the Kingdom – living water that never stops flowing. Your spiritual inheritance is meant to flow through you, to your family, your friendships, your church, your community, to your generation and to those yet to come.

Closing Invitation

Maybe no one told you about your inheritance. But God did. He wrote it in His Word, sealed it with His Spirit and invites you to receive it. Come to His Word. Find your precious promises He has for you. Let them touch your heart and let His spring rise up within you! The river will never run dry!

You are a daughter of inheritance and a part of a story that's still unfolding.

INVITATION TO THE SPRINGS

Chapter 24

Final Blessing

You have an Inheritance

As we draw this journey to a close, let us remember that God's inheritance is everlasting. It did not start with us and it will not end with us.

> For the Lord is good and His love endures forever; His faithfulness continues through all generations.
>
> Ps 100:5 NIV

Psalm 100 is only five verses long, but it echoes with the sound of eternity. It invites us to worship, calls us to serve the Lord with gladness and to remember that we are His people, the sheep of His pasture. But the heartbeat of the psalm is this:

> His faithfulness continues through all generations.

This is our inheritance, the enduring faithfulness of God, flowing like a stream from one generation to the next, from one person to another. Every prayer, every promise, every word you speak. May they bubble up from the depths of your heart, flowing out of your intimacy with the One who loves you, unstoppable and full of life.

Today, as I finish this book, I want to speak directly to you:

> Your inheritance is found in Christ.
> You are His treasure.
> Not because of what you've done,
> but because of who your Father is.
> Because of Jesus.
> Because of the cross.
> Not because you've earned it,
> but because you are loved.
> Simply believe. It's yours.

> I pray the blessing of God over you.
> Over your family.
> Over your friendships.
> Over your calling.
> Over the generations to come.
> May you walk in the fullness of who God has
> created you to be.

May the springs of living water
flow from within you.
May the stones of remembrance
mark your journey.
And may grace tell your story.

The Lord bless you and keep you;
the Lord make His face to shine upon you
and be gracious to you;
the Lord lift up His countenance upon you and
give you peace.

Numbers 6:24–26 ESV

Amen.

Acknowledgements

To those who have stood with me during the writing of this book, I cannot thank you enough. Your prayers and insights have shaped and strengthened these pages more than you know.

I am deeply grateful for the feedback, suggestions and encouragement from family and friends who read the draft. You helped me refine and clarify this work: Darren, Sarah, Anthea, Hannah, Barry, Felicity and Janette.

I thank my husband, Darren and our three children, Tim, Hannah and Josh. They appear here with their permission. I am also grateful to other family members and friends for their willingness to be part of this unfolding story: Jakin, Zoe, Anthea, Judy, Felicity, Lyn, Barry and Judith, Peter and Sarah, Joel and Daniel, and David. Thank you, Yvonne and Sandy, for your godly wisdom woven into this book. These stories have all been used with permission.

Each of you has poured something of yourself into these pages and I pray that this book blesses you.

Throughout this process, I often woke with thoughts I wanted to share with you. My hope is that, as you read these pages, these stories show the inheritance available to you. I pray that the Holy Spirit speaks to your heart about His plans and purposes for you. I know His grace is for you, too!

Rachel

ACKNOWLEDGEMENTS

Endnotes

Discovering Our Inheritance

1. "Strong's Hebrew: 5159. (Nachalah) -- Inheritance, Possession, Heritage, Property." 2025. Biblehub.com. 2025. https://biblehub.com/hebrew/5159.htm.

2. "Strong's Hebrew: 5158. (Nachal) -- Stream, Brook, Valley, Wadi." 2025. Biblehub.com. 2025. https://biblehub.com/hebrew/5158.htm.

Springs in a Dry Land

1. "Topical Bible: Achsah." 2025. Biblehub.com. 2025. https://biblehub.com/topical/a/achsah.htm.

2. "The Spurgeon Library | Achsah's Asking, a Pattern of Prayer." 2020. The Spurgeon Center. 2020. https://www.spurgeon.org/resource-library/sermons/achsahs-asking-a-pattern-of-prayer/#flipbook/.

3. "Strong's Greek: 5. (Abba) -- Father." 2025. Biblehub.com. 2025. https://biblehub.com/greek/5.htm.

4. "Topical Bible: Achsah." 2025. Biblehub.com. 2025. https://biblehub.com/topical/a/achsah.htm.

Courage to Speak Up!

1. Nelson, Thomas. 1994. *Spirit-Filled Life Bible - NKJV*. Thomas Nelson Publishers.

2. "Rest" Ibid., 237.
   "Strong's Hebrew: 5270. (Noah) -- Noah." 2025. Biblehub.com. 2025. https://biblehub.com/hebrew/5270.htm.

3. *Spirit-Filled Life Bible*, Commentary on Numbers 27:1-11.

4. Ibid., 237.

5. Ibid., 237.

6. Ibid., 237.

The God who Sees

1. "Topical Bible: El." 2025. Biblehub.com. 2025. https://biblehub.com/topical/e/el.htm.
   "Topical Bible: Roi." 2025. Biblehub.com. 2025. https://biblehub.com/topical/r/roi.htm.

2. "Genesis 16:13 - the Birth of Ishmael." 2025. Bible Hub. 2025. https://biblehub.com/genesis/16-13.htm.

Encounter at the Well

1. "Lesson 3: The Samaritan Woman (John 4) | Bible.org." n.d. Bible.org. https://bible.org/seriespage/lesson-3-samaritan-woman-john-4.

2. Simmons, Brian. 2023. *The Books of Ezekiel and Daniel*. BroadStreet Publishing Group LLC.

Simple Faith

1. Francisco, Don. 1983. *Give Your Heart a Home*. New Pax Records.

Free Indeed

1. Jayne, Felicity. 2024. *Free Indeed - Finding True Joy*.

Prayer Warrior

1. Elevation Worship and Maverick City Music, and Brandon Lake. 2021. *Talking to Jesus*. Elevation Worship Records.

2. Murdock, Mike . 1982. *Jesus, Just the Mention of Your Name*. 1982 Jim Records.

My Story

1. Frager, Russell. 1998. *Holy Spirit Rain Down*. Hillsong Music Australia.

2. "Ping Pong-A-Thon - Play Table Tennis, Stop Slavery, Free Lives." 2025. Pingpongathon.com. 2025. https://pingpongathon.com.

3. "Vision, Mission & Values - Wycliffe Australia." 2025. Wycliffe Australia. September 3, 2025. https://wycliffe.org.au/about/vision-mission-values.

4. Wycliffe Australia. 2020. "Languages, Languages and More Languages." YouTube. May 20, 2020. https://www.youtube.com/watch?v=_R1ByLkG2Pk.

Our Youngest Olive Shoot

1. Mongomery, Matt. 2010. *Joshua Generation*. https://www.youtube.com/watch?v=A3aoqgTLapQ&t=56s.

The Prodigal's Inheritance

1. Wiersbe, Warren W, and Thomas Nelson. 2019. *Wiersbe Study Bible*. Thomas Nelson.

2. "The Story of the Prodigal | Karen Wheaton Ministries." 2021. Karen Wheaton. April 8, 2021. https://karenwheaton.com/story-of-the-prodigal/.

3. Doss, Lindsey. 2017. *The Way Home*. Independently Published.

4. "Securly - Geolocation Sharing." 2025. Substack.com. 2025. https://lindseydoss.substack.com/p/welcome-to-the-pig-pen.

5. Wickham, Phil , and Brian Johnson. 2020. *Battle Belongs*. Fair Trade Services.

War over the Seed

1. GotQuestions.org. 2020. "Who Was Perez in the Bible? | GotQuestions.org." GotQuestions.org. July 7, 2020.

   https://www.gotquestions.org/Perez-in-the-Bible.html.

2. Cambridge Dictionary. 2025. "Man." @CambridgeWords. September 24, 2025. https://dictionary.cambridge.org/dictionary/english/man.

From Walls to Legacy

1. Wiersbe, The Wiersbe Study Bible: NKJV, Commentary Notes.

Justice in the Shadow of Shame

1. GotQuestions.org. 2020. "Who Was Perez in the Bible? | GotQuestions.org." GotQuestions.org. July 7, 2020.

   https://www.gotquestions.org/Perez-in-the-Bible.html.

2. "Topical Bible: Review of Seal, Cord, and Staff." 2025. Biblehub.com. 2025. https://biblehub.com/topical/s/seal,_cord,_and_staff.htm.

Crowned in Grace

1. "Who Was Bathsheba in the Bible?" n.d. GotQuestions.org.

   https://www.gotquestions.org/Bathsheba-in-the-Bible.html.

2. "Strong's Hebrew: 8010. (Shelomoh) -- Solomon." 2025. Biblehub.com. 2025. https://biblehub.com/hebrew/8010.htm.

3. "Topical Bible: Jedidiah." 2025. Biblehub.com. 2025.

   https://biblehub.com/topical/j/jedidiah.htm.

4. DiMarco, Kristene. 2017. *I Am No Victim*. Bethel Music. https://www.youtube.com/watch?v=eKzhQIE2OM4.

5. "How to Break Free from Victim Mentality." 2025. Charlie Health. May 9, 2025. https://www.charliehealth.com/areas-of-care/trauma/what-is-a-victim-mentality.

Harvesting what she didn't Sow

1. "Ruth 1." 2016. Biblehub.com. 2016. https://biblehub.com/ruth/1.htm.

2. "Ruth 1." 2016. Biblehub.com. 2016. https://biblehub.com/ruth/1.htm.

3. "Strong's Hebrew: 3671. (Kanaph) -- Wing, Edge, Extremity, Corner." 2025. Biblehub.com. 2025. https://biblehub.com/hebrew/3671.htm.

4. Zondervan Bible Publishers (Grand Rapids, Mich. 2017. *NIV Faithlife Study Bible : Intriguing Insights to Inform Your Faith*. Grand Rapids, Michigan: Zondervan.

5. Ibid., 398.

www.ingramcontent.com/pod-product-compliance
Lightning Source LLC
Chambersburg PA
CBHW071955070526
44583CB00015B/1203